Healing Bath Recipes

for the Body,

Spirit, and Soul

Mary Muryn

A FIRESIDE BOOK Published by Simon & Schuster
New York London Toronto Sydney Tokyo Singapore

Water Magic

FIRESIDE
Rockefeller Center
1230 Avenue of the Americas
New York, NY 10020

Fireside and colophon are registered trademarks
of Simon and Schuster Inc.

10 9 8 7 6 5 4 3 2

Designed by BONNI LEON-BERMAN

Manufactured in the United States of America

Library of Congress Cataloging-in-Publication Data
Muryn, Mary.
  Water Magic: healing bath recipes for the body, spirit, and soul /
Mary Muryn.
    p. cm.
  "A Fireside book".
  Includes index.
  1. Baths, Warm—Therapeutic use. 2. Beauty, Personal.
3. Healing. I. Title.
RM822. W2M87 1995
615,8'53—dc20   95–21969
                                                          CIP

ISBN 0-684-80142-6

ontents

Contents

Contents

Part VI

Pleasure and Sexuality Baths 159

Foreword

My mystic friend Mary knows a great many things most of the world doesn't. She has been sharing her wondrous knowledge generously for years with her friends and her clients, and has finally been persuaded to put one small part of her healing grace onto paper so the wider world, too, can benefit from her unique wisdom.

This book uses the medium of the bath as the most pleasurable means possible for healing the body, the psyche, and the spirit. Mary has traveled the world to collect therapies that can transform a simple bathtub into a healing oasis, a ritual temple, or a pleasure spa. There are very few baths in this book that I haven't enjoyed and benefited from—some I feel I couldn't live without.

The finest thing I could wish for you would be to have Mary as your friend. Barring that, it is with the greatest delight that I commend this lovely book to you, in hope that it will entertain, enlighten, and introduce you to an indulgent experience that will provide healing, joy, pleasure, and peace of mind.

CATHY CASH-SPELLMAN

Prologue

The bath can be the one oasis of pleasure and solitude that's always at your fingertips. It can be a time of tranquil refreshment in this frenetic, evermore demanding world.

This book is written to tell you about the extraordinary possibilities for healing, pleasure, beauty, and spiritual growth that baths can provide. Over the centuries, people of wisdom have divined many secrets surrounding the ritual of bathing. There are baths to soothe the emotions, baths to heal illness, and baths to rejuvenate. There are baths with metaphysical properties that can cleanse the aura, open the intuition, clear away negativity, and help the spirit soar.

Come with me on a watery journey of enlightenment to discover the sensual, spiritual, and sybaritic pleasures waiting in your bathtub. I invite you to learn to make a self-indulgent ritual of what may have seemed, up to now, an ordinary, everyday necessity. Once you've let yourself drift into this world of ritual bathing, you may find that your mind eddies out far beyond the bathtub, into the great cosmic ebb and flow of the universe.

Mary's Story

I came from a family that was deeply immersed in the mystery and magic of the Ukraine. Gypsies with crystal balls and tea leaves, earth elementals who lived in the snow-crystal mountains, werewolves and wizards were all part of my ordinary reality.

My own initiation into my special spiritual gifts came at age five, when a golden being appeared in my bedroom. I ran to embrace him and he vanished, but his shimmering memory remained in my consciousness, a harbinger of gifts to come.

By the time I had completed my education in the United States and began teaching college, my life had been guided by many strange metaphysical occurrences. But it wasn't until I met Pat Rodergast, the world-famous channel of the spirit guide Emmanuel, that I accepted the esoteric path I was meant to travel.

Pat told me I was a healer, and that I must prepare myself for the healing work the universe expected of me. So, I began to study, little realizing what an adventurous and circuitous road this would become, and where it would eventually lead.

My Childhood

When I was growing up, I would tell my mother my dreams and she would tell me my future. Of course she was always right, and I grew up thinking that all mothers had her powers.

My father was a bit psychic, also. He told me his destiny was "read" by a famous opera singer, who was a cousin of the czar. She predicted his coming to the U.S. and told him of the main events in his life there. He has another quite useful gift. When playing blackjack he always has a feeling come over him that tells him instinctively which card is coming up next. He loves to gamble occasionally, and when he does he always wins. When I was small, if we were at a fair and there was a prize I wanted him to win for me, he'd simply pick out the number, spin the wheel, and I'd have my doll or stuffed animal. Once we were thrown out of an amusement park for winning too many prizes!

There was always talk in our house of ghosts, and of Gypsies' unerring predictions. Psychic readers were everywhere in the Ukraine. The future was not a mystery—one simply had to ask.

Being brought up entwined in my family's heritage, I didn't discover until college that all the world wasn't like my home. In fact, all my friends wanted me to predict *their* futures and interpret their dreams. It was a part of me to know things others did not know.

My mother's father was an aristocratic landowner. Her grandmother was said to be a psychic and a witch doctor. In my mother's village in the Carpathian Mountains (and in all the surrounding villages) there were many psychics and healers. The people there did not believe in doctors (or have any available to go to); if you were ill, you went to a witch doctor or healer.

Everyone believed in nature spirits. The blades of grass could talk to each other, as did the trees. And all spirits of both the animal and plant kingdoms must be treated with the respect due them as our elder brethren on the planet.

The main healers of the Ukraine were the elder people of the villages. They had old knowledge of flowers, herbs, and roots, and could cure any disease, even cancer. Aloe vera was used as a popular cure for stomach ailments, and every home grew its share.

Most of these people were killed by Stalin and the Russian Revolutionary leaders in the purging of the Ukraine. Sadly, much of their great knowledge has died with them.

EARLY WANDERINGS ON THE PATH

In my early twenties I began a spiritual quest. I wanted to know more about the spiritual and mystical side of life, as my Catholic upbringing left too many questions unanswered. I searched out mystics, shamans, gurus, healers, rabbis, priests—in short, anyone who could guide me on this mysterious journey.

Through years of guided searching and study I learned how to develop my psychic and healing powers; how to open my spiritual energy centers, or chakras, and then release the latent powers within me; and, finally, how to perceive reality's physical, subtle, and causal planes and how to integrate the mind, body, and spirit on these three levels.

Time spent in meditation and Yoga opened all my major senses to the point where my dreams would often predict the next day's events, replete with the exact time of events taking place.

In 1977, my friends told me about a chiropractor/ doctor in New York City who was a powerful healer. I decided to consult with him regarding a neck injury that was causing me a great deal of pain. Although I had seen several specialists without getting relief, he cured me after only three sessions using a combination of chiropractic sacral/occipital techniques (SOT) and vitamin therapy. He explained to me that my energy had to be balanced working with the acupuncture meridians of the body before I could be healed. This had quite a profound effect on me, and I wanted to know everything I could about healing via these mysterious energy currents. He and I became friends, and he opened many doors to the world of natural healing. He took me to alternative medicine conventions, where people such as naturopaths, homeopaths, nutritionists, physicists, medical doctors, and healers all came to share their knowledge with each other. They opened my eyes and mind to a much wider reality than I had dreamed of before.

PAT RODEGAST SEES MY FUTURE

I moved to Westport, Connecticut, in the late 1970s, and shortly after my arrival was introduced to the famous psychic Pat Rodegast, whom I mentioned earlier.

Pat is the author of the best-selling book *Emmanuel,* which is about the channeled wisdom of a disincarnate entity who gives loving and very intelligent advice to us mortals about our place in the universe. Pat travels extensively giving seminars and workshops on spiritual topics.

Once while doing a reading for me, she stopped and looked at me intensely, then said. "What are you doing here! You should be doing what I'm doing!" A few years later, Pat paid me the highest compliment possible by asking me to "read" her on various occasions. She urged me to recognize my powers to heal, as healing was my destiny.

Pat was a wonderful guide and mentor for me, and we both saw clearly the majesty and truth in the mind/body/spirit connection. We started an experimental healing group, working with psychotherapists.

The therapists delved into the psychological areas of the person being healed, Pat would work on the psychic level, and I would work on their bodies, releasing blocked energies that were causing illness or pain. During these sessions, we explored how vital these three aspects of a person's being are in the healing process.

Soon, many, many extraordinary paths opened up to me.

I studied philosophies with every reputable healer I could find: herbology, natural healing, homeopathy, crystals, reflexology, laying on of hands, tarot, astrology, metaphysics, Polarity Therapy. I began to see that each of these philosophies had an important piece of the puzzle to bestow.

The most important of the healers I studied with was Dr. Pierre Pannetier. Dr. Pannetier was the son of a French brain surgeon; his mother was a French/Cambodian Buddhist. During World War II, Pierre was stationed in the South Pacific, where there is a long tradition of witch doctors and shamans. A highly respected shaman recognized in Pierre's aura an unusual power, and predicted he would live through the war and go on to become a great healer.

Unfortunately, due to a severe lack of water, many units in his area of the war were deprived of drinking water, and while at sea the men had to survive for long periods on alcohol. Because of this, his liver was badly damaged, so after the war, he sought out Dr. Randolf Stone, who had founded Polarity Therapy. Dr. Stone not only cured him of his liver ailment and lower-back paralysis through Polarity, but took him on as a student.

Dr. Stone was an osteopath and chiropractor, as well as an ordained minister. He was frustrated by traditional healing methods and by the lack of patient responsiveness to conventional medicine. Dr. Stone began a search for answers that led him to a guru/healer in India, who taught him the Indian Ayurvedic arts, spiritual healing, and how energy works in the body to channel the life force. He then studied Chinese acupuncture, and finally, he combined both Eastern and Western medical concepts into what he called Polarity Therapy—which integrated the body/mind/spirit connection on a very subtle and sophisticated level.

When explaining energy and the healing process, Dr. Stone said "the simple facts are similar to the irrigation of the fields of the earth. The farmer goes along with a shovel and removes the waste that collects in ditches. It is as plain as that, when life is understood." Dr. Stone named Dr. Pannetier as his successor to carry on his teachings when he retired and moved to India.

I studied with the remarkable Dr. Pannetier for six years and became his apprentice. He stayed with me for many extended visits, and I attended his workshops, as both student and assistant. When he retired, he told me he wished me to teach and carry on his work.

At first I practiced on my friends to see how well my healing abilities worked; soon they were sending their friends and families to me. Then doctors and therapists invited me to work with them, and before I knew it, I had a new career.

Yet in my heart, I always knew I was a healer. Ever since I can remember, friends and strangers would come to me for help and advice. Even my parents stopped going to doctors as often, for they said my gifts were better.

In my search for the truth, I have traveled extensively, seeking out shamans and other healers, psychics and prophets, wanting to explore the mysteries hidden in other cultures and religions. I've seen and experienced many wonders in my quest. In Brazil I was put into a trance by a Macumba priest as a form of tribute to my psychic powers. It was a rare honor for an outsider to be permitted to participate in their rituals. In Bali, I observed an entranced healer who cured a woman of paralysis through communication with her ancestors and the gods. For the Balinese, the trance is a part of everyday life. I observed young men put into a trance by temple priests in ceremonies, who became possessed by Ragdah (the most evil witch) so that they pierced their chests with kris swords, but because they were in an altered state, there was no blood, and their cuts healed with unnatural swiftness.

At a fire dance the power of the mind over the body was demonstrated as I watched a village boy in a trance dance over fire without a single burn. The audience actually was burned by the ashes he kicked up, while he danced unscathed through the flames.

I met crystal healers in Brazil and studied with a Cherokee Indian woman who taught me about the rituals of crystals. I studied with a Jain monk (Acharya Sushil Kumaji Maharaj) who taught me much about color therapy, energetic healing, out-of-body travel, visualization, mind power, and how to develop clairvoyance. He was a world leader for peace and head of the peaceful and powerful Jain religion.

I've wandered the world amassing esoteric knowledge from myriad sources, healing and teaching, and now, through this book, sharing what I've learned on a grander scale.

We all have that power to heal—ourselves and others. I offer the knowledge in this book to you in the hope that it may enhance your life and help you take another step along the wondrous road to enlightenment.

ater Meditation

THE HEALING MAGIC OF WATER

Without water our planet has no chance to survive—
without water man is incapable of life. Our very consti-
tution is based upon the need for water. Water
purifies . . . water feeds . . . water sustains all life as we
know it.

This book is a plea to make water sacred once again
on this planet. Look at the joy water brings to human-
ity. Children frolicking in ocean waves at the seashore,
sea shells, and beautifully colored stones washed clean
by the tide, the wondrous coral reefs that are home to
the ocean's denizens. Consider the vast amounts of
oceanic food that has been feeding societies for mil-
lenia.

Water is mysterious.

Siddhartha sat under a tree at the river's edge and
listened to the flow of the water until he realized the
cosmic secrets of the universe the river had to reveal.
Siddhartha became _realized_ at the water's edge. He became the Buddha.

Man has always sought the meaning of life's mysteries, and water is the greatest mystery of all. This book has been conceived to help bring new awareness of a very powerful healing tool that comes right out of your faucet and is always available to you.

Your health is the *most valuable asset* you have. Maintaining this treasure is an ongoing process that demands much more than a yearly check-up. A doctor may tell you your organs are working, but what can he see of your emotions? What can he know of your spirit? Water will help you get in touch with spirit. Your body and mind will surely come into harmony, if your spirit is at peace.

In order to fully experience life, one must allow the spirit to soar—and when the spirit is depressed or discouraged, we must help to revive it. Baths can do this creatively, for water embodies within it many magical healing and life-giving properties. We all know that lack of water brings disease, drought, and starvation to attack the well-being of our planetary neighbors and ourselves.

So let us begin a journey of loving kindness to ourselves. We can make the world a better place through loving ourselves, through taking good care of ourselves. It is the little things that count, and a healing, soothing bath takes very little time and effort, yet gives so much back in return.

Baths: A Brief History

*The way to health is to have an aromatic bath
and scented massage every day.*

—HIPPOCRATES
Greek Physician, Father of Medicine

Since ancient times, bathing has been considered indispensable to emotional and physical health. Hippocrates knew that good health requires both a healthy body and a healthy mind. As far back as 4000 B.C., the ancient Egyptians used bathing as a means of healing the spirit, and certain aromatic baths were believed to produce magical effects on the body.

They discovered that perfumes can profoundly affect a person's emotional and mental states. The Egyptians were very fond of bathing, and perfumed oils were often used in their baths to treat both body and psyche.

Kyphi was the opium of the masses, used as a liquid perfume and known to produce spiritual visions. Plutarch, the great Greek historian, said of Kyphi: "Its aromatic substances lull to sleep, allay anxieties, and brighten dreams. It is made of things that delight most in the night." Kyphi is thought to have been the world's first perfume. The only surviving bottle was discovered in the tomb of Tutankhamen. Remarkably, after 3,300 years it still had a perceptible odor.

Egyptian perfume was as fashionable in ancient Greece as French perfume is now throughout the world. Although the art of making perfumed oils for anointing the body and scenting the bath started in Egypt, the Greeks and Romans raised it to an art form. Caligula spent enormous sums on scented baths, for he believed that aromatic baths could restore a body jaded by sexual excesses.

Before the development of today's sophisticated medicine, people took the matter of health and healing into their own hands. Primitive people's instincts were finely attuned to nature. Just as animals in the wild instinctively gravitate toward the plants that will heal them, so people applied their inner resources to intuit ways and means of healing themselves, using natural responses.

All ancient civilizations had in-depth knowledge of herbs, massage techniques, and bathing therapies that could be used to sustain health.

At the peak of the Greco-Roman civilization baths were celebrated for their majestic splendor and elegance. These grand bathing halls were elegantly designed by the finest craftsmen. Inlaid precious gems and metals dazzled the eye; great works of art were commissioned or brought back as battle spoils. Statues of Hercules, the God of Strength, and of Hygeia, the Goddess of Health, were always present as cosmic overseers of the rites of bathing.

For warriors, the main object of the bath was to provide a means for attaining good health and physical strength. The bath was not merely for luxury or pleasure; it was an integral part of a warrior's rigorous training to prepare for future battles.

Each town had a "Great Bath." People frequented them on a daily basis. There were lecture halls, galleries, and massage rooms, all maintained at public expense.

In Hippocrates' aphorisms, he wrote "Aromatic baths are useful in the treatment of female disorders." He has been dubbed the Father of Holistic Medicine because of his belief in curing his patients with as little discomfort as possible. He advocated the use of massage, music, and perfume as soothing and healing agents, and he also believed that bathing along with drinking wine had curative properties. Needless to say, combining the two has delightful possibilities for soothing the body and the psyche simultaneously.

Today we are beginning to rediscover these ancient pleasures. *Water Magic* will give you guidance on how to proceed on a watery odyssey of healing your mind, body, and spirit.

Peaceful respites from the pressures of life play an important role in well-being. So we invite you to turn inward to create a mood of peaceful solitude that will allow you to go on a wonderful journey. Let your spirit be your guide, with relaxation, rejuvenation, and pure unadulterated pleasure as your goals.

A Few Words Before You Begin

As you read on, you may find baths requiring some exotic ingredients. At the end of this book you'll find resources that will make even volcanic ash available to you—but happily, most of what you'll need is obtainable in your nearest grocery or health-food market.

How to Use the Ingredients in Your Bath Recipes

Oil. For all baths containing essential oils, you may either use the essence alone, or mix it with vegetable oil, honey, or cream. A honey-and-cream bath will have the added benefit of nourishing the skin and giving it a silky feeling. Essential oils do not always dissolve easily in water; mixing them with vegetable oil, honey, or cream will allow them to be dispersed properly by the water, and absorbed better by your skin. Pour the oils into your bath after you have been in it long enough to adjust the temperature. If you pour the oils directly into running tap water, they tend to quickly evaporate.

Bach Flower Remedies. These are natural preparations made from the healing essences of flowering plants and trees. These remedies were discovered, researched, and tested about sixty years ago by noted English scientist and physician Dr. Edward Bach. They dissolve easily into water. As with the oils, put the drops of Bach Flower Remedies into the water after the tub is filled, gently stirring the water with your hands, to disperse the essence into the bath.

Homeopathic Remedies. The form of homeopathic remedy recommended in this book is pellets. They dissolve quickly in warm water.

Herbs, Spices, and Flowers. Whenever an ingredient calls for "steeping," the proper method is to bring a pot of water to a boil on the stove, gently put in the ingredients, and allow them to simmer for twenty minutes, never boiling again. Then add the steeped contents to your tub. One word of caution: don't steep herbs, spices, or flowers in aluminum. Use only ceramic, glass, or metal containers, to avoid altering the therapeutic value of the essence.

A general Shopping and Resource Guide to help you in
obtaining bath ingredients is found on p. 203.

Part I

Emotional Soothing Baths

Bathing Your Emotions

Everything in your environment has a power, or an unseen energy, that surrounds and enlivens it. When our energy field comes into contact with another's energy, we are affected whether we want to be or not. Knowing this, you must develop the fine art of discrimination to protect and guard your precious life force. Discrimination is an artful balancing act. Intelligent, artful discrimination means choosing energies that are compatible with your own—energies that enhance rather than detract from your life.

When you feel out of balance because your energy has been "attacked" by an incompatible force, the bath is a wonderful means of soothing and rebalancing yourself. One of the most comforting sounds in the world is that of gently falling rain against a windowpane. When you hear the gentle pitter-patter of raindrops, suddenly life slows down of its own volition—just as standing under a waterfall can calm and almost magically wash away your cares and tensions. Rain and waterfalls are natural bathers of the auric (your personal energy) field. Fortunately for us, bathing in a bathtub can provide the very same refreshment. The healing properties of water can soothe away your anxieties and gently transport you into a state of deep relaxation.

I offer you my collection of recipes for baths that will do wonders for your sense of well-being. Many of these formulas include herbs and flowers, as they have been proven over the centuries to relax the mind and heal the spirit.

*E*motional Bath Meditation

Once immersed in your bath, gently close your eyes, and let your attention focus sweetly on your breathing. Take ten deep breaths, then allow your mind to relax. Now take some moments to remember a time long ago when you were a child and felt particularly *free*. A time of no cares, and no awareness of the problems of the larger world. Perhaps you were at the seashore, or riding a bicycle, or giggling with your best friend. Concentrate on that moment, try to remember exactly how you felt. Your body was loose and unrestrained, your mind was carefree. Laughter flowed spontaneously from some fountain within. You were totally absorbed in your glee.

Let your whole being drift back, back to this moment, as if you are suspended there, and nothing else exists. *Feel* your joy, the spontaneous, trusting love in your heart, and let yourself imagine life *always* being like that. Relax into it. Let these images rejuvenate your spirit, until you see yourself free and happy. Imagine all obstacles disappearing like mist before the sun. They cannot cling to you, for you are a free spirit, and nothing can stop you from soaring joyously to the heavens.

Drift off to your favorite quiet place in nature. Imagine your guardian angel or spirit guides there with you. *Feel* their protection and love. Allow yourself to be nurtured and taken care of, as you let all your emotional pain be soothed away by their loving presence.

You have the power to transform your life into the images of your most cherished dreams—your imagination has no limitations. So start imagining your perfect life, and let yourself drift off to see where your higher spirit leads you!

OVERVIEW OF
Emotional Soothing Baths

Sleep-Like-a-Baby Bath

- Perfect for when you are overstimulated after a
  hectic day.

Executive-Stress Bath

- This is for stress, insomnia, and high blood pressure.
  It restores balance and harmony.

Restorative Sea Bath

- To revitalize and refresh you, restoring energy.

Opening-Your-Heart Bath

- This helps you to heal emotionally and to rekindle
  feelings of love.

Emotional-Balancing Bath

- This bath greatly soothes and heals the heart.

Sleep-Like-a-Baby Bath

FOR A RESTFUL SLEEP

PURPOSE   When you are overtired or overstimulated, here's a simple way to relax and send yourself off to restful sleep. The preparation for this bath may seem like too much work when you're exhausted, but the ritual of preparation is actually a part of the relaxation process.

1 handful of chamomile flowers
2 chamomile tea bags
Sandalwood incense (optional)
Candles (optional)
1 quart of water

OPTIONAL
8–10 pellets of homeopathic chamomile 30X in the bathwater

HOW TO

Start by steeping chamomile flowers in a quart of water for twenty minutes. During this twenty-minute period, cover your head with a towel and position your head over the stove and inhale the healing aroma of the chamomile steam. Strain and pour the liquid into your bath. Next, using the two tea bags, make yourself a cup of chamomile tea to sip in the bathtub. Steep it lightly and save the tea bags.

Once immersed in the tub, put on some relaxing music. Light the candles and your favorite incense. Close your eyes and place a warm tea bag over each eye. Now imagine yourself drifting off to the seashore, where you are stretched out on the comforting sand. The sun is gently warming your body. Imagine the rolling sounds of the waves as you let yourself drift . . . drift . . .

It is also helpful whenever you are stressed and fatigued to *breathe* deliberately. A simple thing you can do in the tub is put your awareness into your inhalation and exhalation, and at the same time concentrate on your big toes. The big toe is a reflex point in your body for your head. According to the Yogis, energy enters through the head and exits through the feet. This is a good way of "exiting" all your mental stresses and calming your mind. (You can do this exercise in bed, too.)

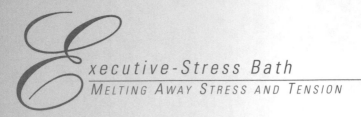

xecutive-Stress Bath
MELTING AWAY STRESS AND TENSION

PURPOSE

This bath is for stress, high blood pressure, and insomnia. It soothes the mind and rejuvenates the heart. It also uses a wonderfully masculine scent, and is very healing for tired, stiff, or overworked muscles.

Lavender was used by the Greeks and Romans to calm wild animals. It acts to calm the aggressive instincts in humans and relaxes the body and mind to induce sleep. Lavender helps bring about a state of peace and can bring over-emotional people under control by connecting their conscious mind with their actions and hearts. Marjoram is superb for treating heart conditions. It has been thought since Roman times that the scent of marjoram promotes longevity. Don't take this bath if you're planning to make love afterward—it's far too relaxing!

5 drops of marjoram (do not overuse, as marjoram is a sedative and can cause drowsiness. Marjoram should not be used by pregnant women.)
10 drops of lavender

HOW TO

Pour the ingredients into a hot tub. Soak in the bath for about twenty minutes. Remember to unplug the phone and put your favorite "unwinding" music on the stereo.

Try to quiet your mind by concentrating on your

breath. Be aware of each inhalation and exhalation. As you begin to relax, become aware of your heartbeat and how its strong, sturdy rhythm replenishes your body's energy. Mentally relax the rest of your body and banish all thoughts of business and stress.

This is a great way to come down from an especially trying day. By giving yourself the gift of tranquillity, you will be strengthened for the fray—when you choose to return to it.

Another exercise you can try:

For an upcoming meeting the next day: imagine yourself at the location of the meeting. (If you've never been there, just imagine the location.) Then visualize the ideal outcome for this meeting, and *not just what you'll settle for!* Feel how you want your business associates and yourself to behave during the meeting as if it were already happening.

See any adversaries as open to you and accepting of your ideas. When you visualize the place for this imaginary meeting, imagine that the energy in there is positive, clean, and harmonious, and that everyone will go home feeling satisfied and happy. Erase whatever blocks you anticipate, then relax and drift.

Visualize in your third eye* the *exact* circumstances

*The spot between and just above the brows that is believed by mystics and Buddhists, Hindus, and so on to "see" beyond the normal senses.

that you need to accomplish; see what you desire in harmony with all those concerned.

Meditate on peace.

Get quiet inside.

Allow the mind to simply *become* quiet.

You can also repeat to yourself the following:

Affirmation

I am at peace.

I have faith in myself and in the universe to achieve my goals.

I have the faith to achieve (or to bring to myself the circumstances that are beneficial to my good.) In my inner dreams I see the accomplishment of all my dreams.

Restorative Sea Bath
REVITALIZING AND REFRESHING AFTER A LONG DAY

PURPOSE   Aphrodite, the Goddess of Love and Beauty, was born in the sea and emerged from the sea foam in a huge shell, which is the symbol for female sensuality.

This bath tones, refreshes, and revitalizes the body, like a dip in the ocean. People have always traveled to the sea to feel young and alive. The sea represents emerging life, as it is believed in many cultures that life originally came from the sea.

The sea has the special ability to heal and rejuvenate both body and spirit. Large bodies of water have a highly charged electromagnetic field around them that create negative ions, which enhance a person's feeling of well-being. Here is the closest thing to recreating the regenerative properties of the ocean in your own home.

1–2 lbs. sea salt
Body brush or loofah

The water shouldn't be too hot, or the bath will tire you out. Find a comfortable warm temperature, put in the salt, and immerse yourself for ten to thirty minutes. Then, with a body brush or loofah, start at your feet and brush or massage your body in an upward direction, toward your head. You'll feel wonderfully rejuvenated.

Optional: After the bath, rinse yourself quickly with a cold shower. This, combined with the salt and scrubbing, will invigorate and regenerate your energy.

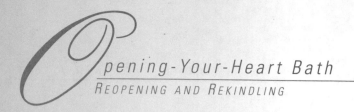

Opening-Your-Heart Bath
REOPENING AND REKINDLING

PURPOSE   This bath is for when your heart feels shut down, closed, and withdrawn (especially from a lover), but you know it's time to reopen your heart to love.

7 drops pure rose oil—Roses have represented love throughout the centuries in many cultures. The inhalation of their scent brings the feeling of love into the heart, and lifts one out of depression.

3 drops lily of the valley oil—Lily of the valley can strengthen the heart and emotions to embrace love without feeling vulnerable.

O PTIONAL

Coconut oil. Mix the lily of the valley and rose oils with a base of coconut oil, and you'll always have lovely soft skin. I have been doing this for fifteen years, and people always comment on the softness of my skin.

Fresh flowers

Pink or aquamarine candles

Uplifting music

HOW TO   For this bath I suggest creating a beautiful atmosphere with fresh, fragrant flowers, pink- or aquamarine-colored candles, and uplifting music, such as Gershwin's *Rhapsody in Blue*.

Once in the tub, allow your senses to speak to you eloquently. Inhale the fragrance of the flowers and let them permeate your entire being. Imagine the fragrance circulating within your body, starting in your heart and spreading outward until you are completely filled with its essence. Listen carefully to the music and let its mood flow through you.

A FFIRMATION

I now welcome love into my life unconditionally and joyously.
I trust in the powers of love.

Practice being in the moment. Feel the heat in your toes, and feel the muscles relax in your feet, and concentrate on how the rest of your body is relaxed as well. Forget the past and the future. Breathe in the *now.* Let the fragrant oils work their magic, and before you know it, your faith in life and love will be restored.

If you wear a pink tourmaline crystal over your heart, it will help heal the pain that is stored there.

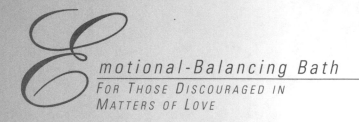

Emotional-Balancing Bath
FOR THOSE DISCOURAGED IN MATTERS OF LOVE

PURPOSE   For matters of the heart, this bath is very healing and soothing. When you have an emotional upset that makes you feel helpless, here is a bath that will heal and deeply soothe your nervous system.

5 drops rose oil
5 drops rosemary oil
5 drops lily of the valley oil
5 drops sandalwood oil
Candles

HOW TO   This is a magic combination. Rose opens the heart and lifts you out of depression; lily of the valley gives the heart strength, both emotionally and physically. These can also be worn together as a perfume on those dog days when life gets you down. Sandalwood calms the nervous system and relaxes the entire body. (And, according to the ancients, it's the only incense pleasing to all the gods.) Rosemary has been used over the centuries in many rituals to attract love. It has the reputation of being a love stimulator.

Before preparing the bath, light some candles and unplug the phone. You can even put a DO NOT DISTURB sign on the door. Once immersed in the bath, concentrate on your breathing and do the Emotional Bath Meditation.

Be aware of your body and your breathing. Feel your heart expand. Imagine there is a prize rosebud in the center of your chest. With your imagination, watch it open slowly and expand, bathing your entire being in loving pink light. Feel the pink light heal your emotions and restore your spirit.

While in the tub inhale the scent of the rosemary and say to yourself: "My relationship with ——— is filled with harmony, understanding, and trust." While filled with the pink rosebud light, imagine the upset in your relationship dissolving and filling with positive warm feelings of understanding, compassion, and love. This love can be with a partner, parent, child, or friend.

Shopping List for Emotional Soothing Baths

You'll want to keep the following on hand, in order to be ready for the moments when emotional replenishment is needed.

HEALTH-FOOD STORE

Body brush, loofa, or sea sponge
Candles
Chamomile flowers
Chamomile tea bags
Chamomile pellets 30X (homeopathic remedy)
Incense (your favorite, or sandalwood)
Sea salt

ESSENTIAL OILS

Lavender oil
Lily of the valley oil
Marjoram oil
Rose oil
Rosemary oil

MUSIC

Your Choice
Rhapsody in Blue

Part II

Homeopathic Baths

The Law of Similars

Two hundred years ago in Germany, a brilliant and renowned physician, Samuel Hahnemann, lost his beloved seven-year-old daughter in an epidemic. Grieving and enraged at the failure of the medical profession to save her, he vowed he would never again practice medicine until he'd found a better method.

Hahnemann spoke seventeen languages and earned his living, for a time, translating medical texts into, and out of, German. While working on a treatise on malaria, he noticed that the symptoms produced when a healthy person swallowed quinine (the cure for malaria) were nearly identical to the symptoms of malaria itself. From this insight, he evolved the hypothesis that *like cures like.* For example, a substance which produces a sore throat can be used to cure a sore throat. He called this the Law of Similars.

Dozens of doctors and students who loved and respected Dr. Hahnemann worked with him on "provings," which were experiments with vast numbers of substances that would validate his hypothesis. Over time, he realized that even the most minute quantity of a given substance possessed the "energy" of that substance. Based on these findings, homeopathic remedies use incredibly tiny amounts of the "like" substance, so they are safe and easy to work with and can be purchased without a prescription.

Recent experiments in France have suggested that the homeopathic remedy, even in its minutest dose, may actually change the molecular structure of the water, "potentizing" it energetically in some as yet not understood way.

BACH FLOWER REMEDIES

These "flower-powered" remedies are based more on psychological symptoms than physical ones, and are not prescribed in the same way as homeopathic remedies. They were developed by the British homeopath and bacteriologist Edward Bach, who intuited a system that cataloged thirty-eight different emotional states. He then found flower essences that worked with these different emotional states to help cure imbalances in subtle, energetic ways.

Rescue Remedy is the most popular and universally recognized of the Bach Flower Remedies. It greatly reduces the emotional trauma connected with emergency situations such as accidents, fires, or extreme stress. Rescue Remedy helps a person's energy return to normal (it is no substitute for medical care when needed). I've used Rescue Remedy during frightening cab rides in New York City, or during a treacherous ride through a blizzard in upstate New York.

ealing Meditation
How to Release the Repetitious Patterns That Hold Us Back

The first thing that you want to address is whether you want to stop or cure your addiction to the pattern.

Like any addiction, whether it is drugs, alcohol, tobacco, or coffee, people get a certain pleasure from the suppression, from the suffering—from closing off their energies. Any of these negative patterns actually close off your energy field, and this closing off all comes from one source, which is fear. Fear is the basis of every addiction, because we are frightened of what will happen to us if we allow ourselves to be expanded. If we are really open and visible, we are vulnerable, so people keep themselves closed down and in the background, so as not to be hurt any further by life. It's easier to stay *in the pattern* than to risk the greater pain of freedom from it.

What is needed to go forward is *courage*. Courage has to be found within, and *finding* your courage is a process of self-discovery. Ask yourself "Where is my courage? Where does it reside inside of me? Where did it go? How did it get diminished?" You'll be surprised at the answers that will surface. We need the courage to get beyond the fear.

Think of the courage of a soldier or warrior who risks death to achieve victory. That is the kind of courage you need to invoke in yourself. This is a wonderful time to pray to that higher source, to God or the various gods, prophets, or saints who have meaning for you. Ask them to give you back your courage.

AFFIRMATION
When you want to break a pattern, invoke courage:

God please make me strong enough.
Please make me fearless.
Please give me the courage to accomplish
my goal.

Visualize accomplishing your goal—creating a healthy, loving relationship; receiving proper remuneration for your work efforts, so you are not underpaid, manipulated, or used; not choosing bosses who will never see or bring out your full potential. You need courage to go forth into life and into the world, to experience it in a deeper way. And in order to experience life more deeply, you need passion.

Do you know people who are totally passionless? They seem very stoic and very limited in their interaction with life. They have limiting beliefs, narrow sets of rules and regulations by which they live their lives. They are devoid of passion. Now create in your mind the fantasy image of a painter, an artist—someone like

Dali or Van Gogh, someone who followed his passion and imagination in every act of his life. Some creative people have taken their passion to the point of insanity. But what we want to capture is that fervor, the freedom, the spontaneity, for this is the essence of what you need to capture for yourself.

And once you trust that *essence,* and give yourself the freedom to follow your passion, you will achieve everything you want in life.

OVERVIEW OF
Homeopathic Baths

Battered-Body Bath

- Arnica for physical shock and pain.

Emotional-Pain Bath

- Rescue Remedy for emotional trauma and upset.

Clean-Up-Your-Heart Bath

- Crab apple for emotional cleansing.

Live-in-the-Moment Bath

- Releasing emotional ties to the past.

Get-Moving Bath

- Chestnut Bud Bath, to stop spinning your wheels and let your energy flow.

Battered-Body Bath
ARNICA FOR PHYSICAL SHOCK AND PAIN

PURPOSE   Arnica, a staple homeopathic remedy, is a great healer for sprains, bruises, pain, and aching muscles. It alleviates the bodily shock from anything, from accidents to going to the dentist. Arnica greatly speeds up the healing process, and reduces swelling from bruises, bumps, and sprains.

8–10 pellets of arnica 30X dissolved in the bath

HOW TO   Soak for ten to thirty minutes as needed. Try to relax as much as possible. This takes a while to work, and the strongest results will probably be felt a few hours *after* the bath. But there will be some instant relief with the hot water.

This bath can be taken repeatedly (one to three times a day) until the condition disappears. Don't underestimate the subtlety of this remedy—it is very powerful and consistent in its healing power.

Arnica is often prescribed by homeopathic physicians to be taken internally in pellet form, depending on the type and severity of the injury. You can safely take a few of the arnica pellets two to three times a day without taking a bath. And don't forget the power of your mind in the healing process. *Visualize yourself healed!*

I recommended this bath to a friend of mine in the moving business. His back constantly ached due to all the heavy lifting. He calls it his "miracle bath," for he no longer lives with constant pain. If he has a rough day, he knows just what to do.

motional-Pain Bath
RESCUE REMEDY FOR EMOTIONAL TRAUMA AND UPSET

This bath can prove to be invaluable in cases of shock or trauma. Whether from an accident or from emotional upset, this bath will calm you and stabilize you. It works equally well for people of all ages—infants to elderly. It is a very calming, soothing, healing way to deal gently, but effectively, with trauma. Rescue Remedy should always be kept on hand.

PURPOSE

10 drops of Rescue Remedy (5 drops in the bath, 5 drops in a glass of water)

Add the Rescue Remedy to a tub of hot water and soak as long as necessary (ten to thirty minutes). Also, while in the tub, have a glass of cool water with five drops of Rescue Remedy in it and sip while bathing.

HOW TO

You'll be surprised at how quickly you'll feel better. This is also a great bath for those nights when your troubles are keeping you awake. It will calm your anxiety. Just bring your glass of water into the bedroom, take a few sips every time you wake up, and soon your mind will be at peace.

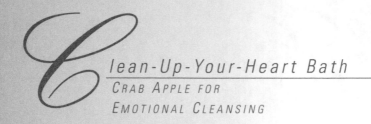

Clean-Up-Your-Heart Bath
CRAB APPLE FOR
EMOTIONAL CLEANSING

PURPOSE   Crab apple, in the form of a Bach Flower Remedy, is healing for those feeling tainted, molested, or abused. It is for times of low self-image or low self-esteem. Crab apple helps to clean these feelings out of one's inner space, and out of the auric field.

Oil of crab apple was used initially to anoint and purify love altars. Your body is your temple and anointing it with crab apple oil purifies and cleanses it of pain and trauma.

10 drops Crab Apple Bach Flower Remedy
Washcloth

HOW TO   Fill the tub with hot water. After shutting off the water, pour in the crab apple and swirl the drops around the tub with both hands. Slowly get into the tub and relax. Soak a washcloth with the bathwater, fold it, and place it over your eyes.

Concentrate on feeling the emotions flowing within you. Start mentally listing your positive qualities, as you let the warm water release your tensions. Don't give time to negativity. When a negative thought pops up, wash it away with a swish of your hand through the water around your body.

Imagine you are at a holy temple on an island in the middle of the sea. It is a glorious, warm, sunny day.

Your soul is soothed by the peaceful calm of the sea's waves.

With a reverence for the sacredness of the moment, recall one by one the events causing you your pain. If you have been abused or molested, get in touch with where you store your guilt and shame inside your body.

Keeping your breath concentrated on these areas, consciously release any responsibility you feel you have for causing these incidents to occur. With your strongest powers of visualization and concentration, forgive yourself and then dissolve the past. Imagine the divine powers of grace at this holy temple are releasing your past. *Let it go!*

Relax quietly for a few moments, then wholeheartedly connect to your goodness and the things you love about yourself. If any contradictory thoughts come up, banish them.

AFFIRMATION

I am a child pure and free. My heart leads me to my destiny. I am safe and I am protected. There is a circle of light that encompasses me and connects me to the goodness, abundance and love of the Universe.

Do this bath once a week until your healing feels complete.

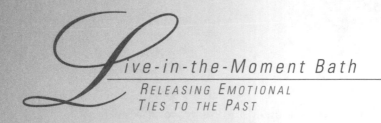

*L*ive-in-the-Moment Bath
RELEASING EMOTIONAL
TIES TO THE PAST

PURPOSE   All of us have experienced a time when letting go of
someone was for the best—but very difficult to do *from
the heart.* It could be an old love gone bad—or a current
one that is destructive. Sometimes we need to let go of
a person who has passed on, or parents who affected
us in a negative way. The walnut bath helps you to release old ties, so new, more positive ties have room for
growth. Walnut trees have been respected throughout
modern history for their beauty and fruit. Witches used
to dance under the walnut trees to aid fertility. Walnut
promotes new beginnings, on all levels of person's being. It aids change and positive growth, and is considered a forceful healing potion.

*10 drops Walnut Bach Flower Remedy, or,
6 walnuts boiled in a pot (not aluminum) for 3 hours, starting
with a quart of water and adding more when necessary*

HOW TO   It is important to know that you should take this
bath seriously. If done properly, it will sever your emotional ties to another person. *Make sure that this is what
you truly want* and that it is the best thing for you.

Don't ever do this bath out of anger. Try to do it out
of love for yourself, and your healing process. Think of
the person you need to let go of and imagine you are
releasing him/her to follow his/her highest destiny in

this life. Let go of your pain and anger. Imagine all ties and cords being severed, and see yourself freed to search for your true love, and your true happiness in this life.

Stay in this bath for as long as you feel necessary. If you wish, you can also take a few drops of the Walnut Remedy in a glass of water before you retire. Repeat this bath often until the bond is truly broken, but if you find yourself getting too emotional, slow down and do the bath less frequently.

While in the Bath

Imagine a walnut in its shell; the meat is a seed. Imagine yourself inside this shell as if it were a womb—and in this seed is embodied all the potentials of your life, everything you can imagine that you want to do, to achieve.

You are going back in time—going back to the seed of your life, that seed that embodies all possibilities. Nothing is in that seed that can stand in your way.

Go to the beginning and imagine everything that your dreams can allow—your happiness, the love in your life, your creative achievements, your health, your loving relationships, your prosperity—everything that would give you the most enriched life. Imagine that everything available in the universe for human development is available right now in that seed. Imagine that the seed expands and strengthens to the point where the shell is no longer necessary. The seed begins to grow outside of the shell. And in this seed, in this energy that is you, imagine your energy expanding in every direction, like the spokes in a bicycle wheel emanating in all directions, like a wheel of life that will be the manifestation of your existence. And in this wheel and spokes are every accomplishment that you can envision—they embody everything that is the fulfillment of you.

In this expansion, you erase those things that are truly your obstacles—your fear, your pain, your anxiety—that you have been programmed with from the beginning. You are actually going to be *reprogrammed* with a new consciousness, into the vision of light rather than the vision of darkness. You are erasing all the dark parts of your life and you are releasing the past and saying, "I am now being born anew, I am now *creating* my life afresh."

After your bath you may want to write in a "stream-of-consciousness" journal all that comes to you after this meditation, as an added way of letting go and affirming your dreams of a happy future.

Keep track of your dreams after doing this bath. Have a pen and pad by your bedside, as your subconscious may let you know if you've been successful, or give you some other important messages.

Get-Moving Bath
LETTING YOUR ENERGY FLOW

Stop spinning your wheels and get out of your rut. **PURPOSE**
When you become aware that you repeat the same mistakes in your life over and over, you're also smart enough to know better. Some common areas where being in a rut can keep you from progressing are love, money, business, career, and health.

20 drops Chestnut Bud Bach Flower Remedy

This bath releases the locked energy patterns in your **HOW TO**
body and psyche that are causing you to do things to escape from yourself, rather than facing the problems in your life and changing them.

While soaking in the Chestnut Bud bath, think about a recurring negative pattern in your life that is preventing you from achieving happiness and fulfillment. Then imagine that you have the vision and wisdom to transform this situation into one based on truth and clarity. Invoke your inner vision so you can clearly see the "hook" that snares you into this pattern, and then magically make the hook disappear into the air, never to come back.

If you're working on a specific problem, do this bath once or twice a week until you see a breakthrough in your personal life.

Shopping List for Homeopathic Baths

Preparations

Arnica—homeopathic pellets
Chestnut Bud Bach Flower Remedy
Crab Apple Bach Flower Remedy
Rescue Remedy
Walnut Bach Flower Remedy, or real walnuts

Part III

Healing Baths

Accessing the Power Within

Can bathing in a "substance" actually heal an internal problem? If that notion seems far-fetched to you, consider the efficacy of the Epsom salts bath for muscle strains or sprains that athletes have used for generations. And don't forget external poultices and ointments that have been used for a variety of ailments for centuries. Even though they are applied to the outside of the body, their results occur within.

After all, science considers the skin to be the largest organ of the body. So essential is it as a conduit from outside the body to its inside functions that if this organ's breathing or waste excretion capacity is inhibited, a person can die as a result.

In France, the work of Maurice Messengue has received considerable notice. He is a botanist and herbalist who has used herbal foot- and hand-baths to cure an astonishing array of illnesses for many people, including popes and presidents.

The following chapter is a compendium of healing baths compiled from a myriad of sources, from Native American sweat lodges to the healing waters of European spas, from the magic cauldrons of the ancient druids to the volcanic ash collected in South Sea island paradises. Each of these baths can help to heal the body, creating an environment that will revive the spirit as well.

These baths will help you tap the *power within* in order to access the great energies within you that can heal your pain, and restore your sense of well-being.

The baths in this chapter have been proven to work. It is important to realize that when there is pain or sickness, *we can do something about it,* and we don't always have to rely on outside sources to make us better. Taking an active role in our own healing process is an affirmation of our intention to restore health and balance to our bodies, minds, and souls.

Good-Health Meditation

It is important to realize that there is a connection between emotional and physical sickness. Sadly, many people have a stronger affirmation for death than for life.

What is your commitment to your *aliveness?* To what extent are you willing to be alive—to experience *life?*

Some of us live our lives in an almost crippled way. Every week there seems to be a new ailment, sickness, or disease. Others seem to be healthy, no matter what. Health comes from the commitment to one's aliveness—and the willingness to *breathe* in the life force, the energy that permeates our life force, breathe it into our physical body and allow it to energize us. Breath is important to health; it is connected to the Great Breath of the Universe. Be aware of the times you are not feeling well, and you will realize that you are not really breathing very much either. That's why many people feel that Yoga and Tai Chi promote longevity, because these arts are doing something to connect people *consciously* to their breath. Health is a full-time job—it takes awareness and discipline and commitment.

Think of the things that you eat, and the other substances that you ingest, and make a commitment to health and well-being with every food or beverage.

A F F I R M A T I O N

> *Think:*
> *I am happy and alive in every aspect of my being.*
> *My cells are healthy and strong.*
> *My organs work easily at full capacity.*

Go through the different parts of your body and enliven them by breathing life into them. Where there is pain, talk to your pain. How connected are you to your body, how often do you talk to it, and how much time do you spend listening to it? Many times we hear people say, "My body was telling me to slow down, but I just didn't listen." It's important to start listening.

While you are doing the baths in these chapters, take the time to listen and speak to your body. Take the time to breathe and use the power of your mind to visualize yourself making a total commitment to your health and well-being. Remember, a positive attitude toward life is the single most powerful medicine.

Healing Baths

Healing-Colds-and-Flu Bath
- For colds and flu.

Chinese-Ginger Bath
- For colds, flu, aches and pains.

Joyful-Joints Bath
- For arthritis and rheumatism.

Help-for-Headaches Bath
- For healing an aching head.

For-Women-Only Bath
- For female problems and infections.

Sea-Essence Bath
- Mineral Purifier–Detox.

Horrible-Hangover Bath
- Bathtub gin, to help after overindulgence.

Aztec-Secret Bath
- For curing exhaustion.

Wonderful Weight-Loss Bath
- To take pounds away.

PURPOSE   This bath helps to eliminate mucus in the upper respiratory system, while improving circulation and helping to relieve head pain. A hot bath can actually help a sinus headache or a stuffed nose. Dr. Lloyd Rosenvold, a noted physician, has researched the effects of hot water on the feet and has discovered that the hot water makes the blood vessels in the feet open up wider than usual. Blood then rushes in to fill the enlarging arteries and is drawn from the head, which unclogs the nasal passages.

According to the *Prevention How-To Dictionary of Healing Remedies and Techniques* (Rodale Press, 1992), another researcher who has worked extensively in this field, Dr. Richard Hansen, found the following: "Besides soothing nerves, muscles, and joints . . . hopping into a hot bath at the first sign of sniffles might help drain away a cold or flu. 'A hot bath or shower that increases body temperature to 103°F has been shown to increase the infection-fighting white blood cell count three-fold for 5 hours,' says Dr. Hansen. 'What's more, most cold and flu viruses don't multiply at temperatures above 101.6°F.' "

5 drops of eucalyptus oil (to open up the nasal passages)
5 drops of peppermint oil (to invigorate the body)
5 drops of lavender (this has the ability to stimulate the white
  blood cells to combat infectious bacteria)
2 tbsp. of vitamin C crystals.
8 drops of thyme (or a handful of fresh steeped thyme) if your
  chest is also congested; this also raises the immune system

Soak for as long as you are comfortable. It is impor-   HOW TO
tant to relax. Put a DO NOT DISTURB sign on the
door, shut off the phone, and drink plenty of hot water
with lemon and honey.

Afterward, watch a funny movie to take your mind
off your discomfort, and then go to sleep.

You can take a second bath with ginger,
later in the day, to pull out additional mucus from your system. It's always best to
take the ginger bath in the evening.

Before you go to sleep, put a few
(three or four) drops of eucalyptus
oil on the edge of your pillow. This has
been known to dry up colds overnight.

Make sure it is in a section of your pillow that does not touch your skin. Eucalyptus oil
comes in a light or clear form to avoid staining your
linens.

Chinese-Ginger Bath
FOR COLDS, FLU, ACHES AND PAINS

Ginger has a long history of medicinal use in China, where they drink ginger tea to cure colds, the flu, and other ailments.

PURPOSE   This bath has worked for many of my most skeptical clients, and they are devoted to it. It is great for when your joints act up, or when you have a persistent pain. It is also beneficial for colds, flu, sciatica, aching muscles, and arthritis.

1 oz. powdered ginger

OPTIONAL
Fresh ginger root for tea

HOW TO   Pour ¾ to 1 oz. bottle of powdered ginger into your bathwater. If you have sensitive skin, start with ½ oz. and increase after five minutes. You should feel a slight tingle around the genital area. Soak for twenty minutes. You will feel your entire body heat up, and a strong healing warmth will soak into your joints. For severe cases of arthritis, take a fifteen-second cold shower after the bath to lock the ginger heat into your joints.

In cases of colds or flu, the ginger will send warmth throughout your entire body and help you to sweat out toxins. If you feel shaky or dizzy, get out of the tub, for ginger has served its purpose.

And, while you're bathing, don't forget the power your mind has to heal you. The powers of positive thinking, visualization, and prayer can be most helpful to your process.

A Hand- and Foot-Bath:

Soak hands and/or feet in bowls of ginger and hot water for twenty minutes, then rinse in cold water.

After the bath, get into bed under the covers, and let your body rebalance itself. If you want, put on a guided meditation healing tape.

Ginger Tea:

You will never have another sore throat if you use this remedy. At the first hint of soreness, cut three or four slices of fresh ginger root (about the thickness of a nickel) and put them into a pot with three cups of water. Bring this to a boil, then simmer for twenty minutes. Add honey to taste, and drink one cupful. Or drink several cupfuls throughout the day.

*J*oyful-Joints Bath
COMFREY AND CHAPARRAL

PURPOSE   This is a great all-around healer and rejuvenator for the joints, as well as being especially good for arthritis and rheumatism.

3 drops of eucalyptus oil (optional as an anti-inflammatory oil)
1 handful of comfrey leaves
2 handfuls of chaparral herb (specific for joints and rheumatism)

OPTIONAL
Make yourself a cup of tea using ½ tsp. of comfrey and ½ tsp. chaparral
Use a little honey for flavoring

HOW TO   Comfrey is often called "bone set" or "knit bone," as it has been used medicinally for over two thousand years to heal fractures and wounds.

The healing substance in comfrey is allantoin, which helps the body protect itself by replacing cells after an operation or injury.

An ointment can be made from the freshly grated comfrey root (combined with a little water) that will ease burns. Cuts and scrapes can be healed with comfrey tea (from fresh leaves) poured onto cotton pads and applied to the skin.

In the bath, the body absorbs the healing properties of comfrey.

During the Middle Ages, monks were often considered healers. They always had comfrey growing in their gardens, for use in healing the sick and injured. (A popular myth during that time was that comfrey mixed into the bath would restore a woman's virginity.)

Steep, in hot water, a combination handful of comfrey and chaparral for twenty minutes, then strain and pour into a hot tub. Soak for twenty to thirty minutes, feeling your joints unkink and relax.

Comfrey and chaparral make a wonderful healing tea when sweetened with honey. Drink it during your bath, or in the morning when you wake up.

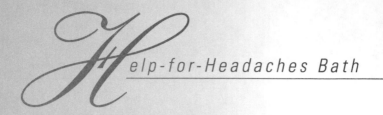# elp-for-Headaches Bath

PURPOSE   This bath opens your pores to allow blood and oxy-
gen to circulate through your head to alleviate
headaches. Varying scents must be used for different
types of headaches.

*2 drops of peppermint oil on a compress for the forehead, or
5 drops for the bath, can be used for* any headache
*2 drops of lavender oil on a compress for the forehead, or 5
drops for the bath,* for a neck tension or eye strain headache
*2 drops of chamomile oil on a compress for the forehead, or 5
drops for the bath, for either a* gastric or nervous tension
headache

OPTIONAL
add 3 drops of eucalyptus oil for a sinus headache

HOW TO   Before you begin your bath, rub a small amount of
lavender oil on the back of your neck. Soak in a hot water bath, and put a towel filled with ice on your forehead or around your head. Massage around your
temples and the base of the skull with two fingers. Put
one drop of the oil appropriate for the type of
headache you have on each finger.

Breathe in slowly through your nose, and release your breath through your mouth. Visualize the air you breathe in to be white and clear, and the released breath to contain all your pain and negativity. See it evaporating into the sky. Try to rest after the bath.

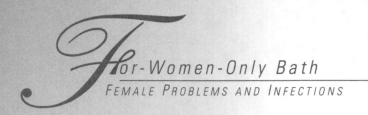

For-Women-Only Bath

FEMALE PROBLEMS AND INFECTIONS

PURPOSE   This bath works for vaginal infections, including yeast, bladder infections, cysts, and problems with the reproductive system. It helps to rebalance hormones and the monthly cycle. Use this bath when you have any sort of infection; it will help heal it, and will have a calming effect on your entire body.

A handful of each of the following, steeped like tea, and poured through a tea strainer, in 2 quarts of water for 20 minutes:
Sage
Thyme
Rosemary
Whole cloves

HOW TO   Strain the tea and pour the liquid into a bathtub full of water. It may turn the water a little brown, but that's okay. Relax for twenty minutes.

While soaking in the tub, think of any disturbing emotional situation in your present life—usually a love relationship—and evaluate whether that could be causing you to close down emotionally or sexually. Is there any current sexual guilt, or unresolved issues you have with the men in your life? Take a good look inside, and you may be surprised how connected your problem in the relationship is to your present physical problem.

Sometimes, you may get a bladder infection from a night of wonderful, prolonged, intense sex. This bath can help alleviate the problem, leaving you with only the happy memories to enjoy.

For those who want to try an old-fashioned remedy that always works, take a peeled clove of garlic and place it in your vagina overnight. This works best when you make a vaginal suppository out of cotton soaked in cold-pressed olive oil with the garlic wrapped up inside. No need to worry about the garlic smell—there is no detectable odor! This has cured my worst infection in two to three nights. A clove of garlic also brings on those late periods—thus alleviating your PMS problems.

This bath can also be used as a foot bath or hand bath for infections to those parts of the body.

*S*ea-Essence Bath
MINERAL PURIFIER-DETOX

PURPOSE   To detox the body of impurities that can slow us
down. Seaweed is rich in minerals like magnesium,
potassium, iron, and zinc that are super-cleansers of
toxins. Seaweed also has antibiotic properties.

½ lb. French freeze-dried seaweed
10 drops of favorite essential oil

OPTIONAL
Mix seaweed with water into a paste and put it on your face
  as a mask to rejuvenate it while bathing

HOW TO   Health, invigoration, and aliveness are the things
you need to think about in this bath. Think about the
powers in the sea and the life that is born from the sea,
the many types of food it provides, fish, algae, and so
on. The sea is abundant and rich, and is a great source
of life. This life force that the sea embodies enters into
you during this sea bath. You want to feel the life force
rushing in and the toxins, imbalances, and impurities
being pushed out—the sea is flushing them away. It is
caressing your nerves, just as the gentle waves do at the
seashore. Feel as if your heart is being invigorated by
the cool breezes. Imagine this as you are in your bathtub . . . the fresh cool air, the warm sunshine. Imagine
yourself expanding into the beauty of the seashore, getting lighter and lighter, with all your cares being
washed away . . . floating in freedom, and every cell of

your being undergoing rejuvenation. The purpose of
your sea bath is rejuvenation of mind, body, and spirit.
Also, if you mix some of the seaweed into a paste, you
can put it on your face to rejuve-
nate it while bathing.

Horrible-Hangover Bath
Bathtub Gin

Purpose   This is for the morning after a night of indulgence.

> *5 drops of fennel oil*
> *3 drops of juniper oil*
> *8 drops of rosemary oil*
> *2 tbsp. vitamin C in crystal form*
> *Juice of ½ lemon in cup of hot water*

How to   After you fill your bathtub with water, pour in all the ingredients and swish the water thoroughly. Since alcohol deprives the body of life-giving water through dehydration, this bath is a great way to restore it to balance. Have a glass of hot water and lemon juice to sip slowly while in the tub, and put a compress of the bathwater solution over your forehead.

It's well-known that in the Roaring Twenties, bootleggers used to make illegal liquor in their bathtubs, called "Bathtub Gin." What's less well-known is that during Prohibition, the bathtub was also used as a means of getting rid of hangovers through relaxation.

To use this bath to rid yourself of a hangover, you must first become aware of your breathing for a few minutes. When you have reached a state of profound relaxation, get in touch with your power and will. Send healing energy to those parts of your body that are out of balance. We all have the power to heal—our cells have an inner intelligence that knows how to heal and rebuild. Use your imagination as creatively as a child would. See yourself well and energized—laughing and playing, enjoying the pleasures of life fully. Keep only positive thoughts and emotions flowing through you, and dissipate the negative ones as if by magic.

Now let yourself just drift, relax, and feel better.

Aztec-Secret Bath
FOR CURING EXHAUSTION

PURPOSE   This bath is perfect for those times when you are totally exhausted, but you have an important day or evening ahead of you.

Aztec Secret (1 cup Indian healing clay, found in the health food store)
1 cup of peppermint tea to sip while in the bath

HOW TO

Soak in the clay bath for twenty to thirty minutes. This will totally rejuvenate you.

Clay has played an integral role in beauty baths and masks throughout the centuries. Over five thousand years ago, clay from the Nile and the Arabian desert was used by Cleopatra in her daily beauty ritual.

Famous spas in Germany and Italy (some going back four thousand years to Roman times) have been using clay packs and overall clay treatments to beautify and to heal. Many renowned naturopaths such as Kneipp, Vuhn, and Just have relied on clay for their natural elements.

While soaking, try to relax your mind. Let it wander to pleasant thoughts, feelings, and memories. If a negative thought crops up, put a bubble of white light around it and gently visualize it floating out of your field of inner vision. See it dematerialize. Play some uplifting music, and enjoy a cup of peppermint tea.

If you can, swiftly rinse your body in cool water. If that is unappealing, try lukewarm water.

You can also make a mask for your face with Aztec Secret. This will re-energize your skin, and make tired lines disappear for the evening. Simply mix some Aztec Secret with water or vinegar into a paste, and apply it to your face and neck. Always avoid the eyes! This will act as a mini-face-lift! Apple cider vinegar mixed with clay was a healing poultice developed by a sixteenth-century priest from the South of France, who gained acclaim as a result.

One wonderful way to cure exhaustion is through laughter. Take a comic book into the tub to get some humor into your life. Think of funny moments in the past. Humor releases stress, and most of our exhaustion is caused by stress. So start with humor—put on a tape of your favorite comedian, and laugh your cares away in the tub.

onderful Weight-Loss Bath
TO TAKE POUNDS AWAY

PURPOSE   These oils will improve body-tissue tone and help "attack" the fat in your cells.

5 drops grapefruit oil
5 drops lemon oil
5 drops sage oil
5 drops basil oil

HOW TO   Mix all the oils into your bathwater. Give yourself a good invigorating massage with a loofa sponge while in the tub. Also massage the acupressure reflex point for the thyroid, at the base of each big toe, for two to three minutes. Afterward, relax and use the power of your mind to visualize your perfect body. If you care to, get a picture of yourself or a model with your ideal body type. Look at it while in the tub and imagine your body transformed into this new one.

You may be surprised to find some hidden resistance come up while visualizing your new body—reasons that you are keeping yourself over-weight. A friend of mine kept herself fat because otherwise she could never say no to men when pursued sexually. Another woman harbored anger at her husband, and this was her way of punishing him. A beautiful teenage girl I know gained a great deal of weight after being sexually abused by her mother's boyfriend.

There are a great many reasons why people are overweight besides the fact that eating is fun, pleasurable, and necessary. There has been much research done on food allergies causing people to be overweight. We usually crave the food we are most allergic to. Eliminating that food from your diet for eight weeks is one way to curb the allergy.

Open your mind and try to discover the emotional and/or physical conditions that are causing you to be overweight.

Weight-Loss Bath Meditation:

First of all, what is needed is a positive mental attitude about one's body, about how you feel about yourself. It's not about how many pounds your body weighs, but the heaviness of the feelings inside that you harbor about yourself. That is the most important weight that needs to be lifted—the weight of the negative feelings that you harbor within you.

When you are in this bath, mentally note these negative feelings, explore them, don't judge them—but seek them out, and in your infinite inner truth, discover what you *really* think about your body. Your feelings come from way back. It could be something that someone said ages ago that stuck with you. Perhaps this person was an authority figure when you were very young. To release the past, you want to be in the present moment—but it is necessary and okay to explore the past as long as you stay in the present. You want to take the negative feelings, erase them, and imagine the opposite being true. The heaviness is our inner heaviness, our inner pain—and the pain we may be carrying for others. We also sometimes need protection because of your sensitivity to the world, and our excess weight is our armor.

The condition of being overweight can be traced to something as simple as *fear* . . . fear of being everything that we can be. The way our body *is* may simply be the way our body is supposed to be in this lifetime, and if that's what your heart tells you, then you need to accept that fact unconditionally. But, if you are using weight to hide out from your fear—or because of low self-esteem—then you need to look very honestly at yourself, and do this bath two to three times a week. Let it be a time of exploration. Don't judge yourself by the thoughts that you have harbored all along—begin by exploring your feelings instead. Do this exploration process as a separate meditation outside the bath. The most important component of your meditation needs to be self-love and self-acceptance.

A F F I R M A T I O N

I love myself, and I accept myself, totally the way I am *at this moment in time.*

As your body changes, love it and accept it that way too. But remember, you need to accept it the way *it is,* in order to have a solid foundation from which to change.

Shopping List for Healing Baths

HEALTH-FOOD STORE

Aztec Secret (volcanic ash)
Chaparral leaves
Cloves (whole)
Comfrey leaves
Freeze-dried seaweed
Ginger powder
Ginger root
Rosemary leaves
Vitamin C

ESSENTIAL OILS

Basil oil
Eucalyptus oil
Fennel oil
Grapefruit oil
Juniper oil
Lavender oil
Lemon oil
Peppermint oil
Sage oil and powder or leaves
Thyme oil and powder or leaves

Part IV

Metaphysical Baths

The Body Electric

Imagine, for a moment, that you are not merely the physical body you see, but that you are also a glowing grid of electrical energy currents. Then imagine that the acupuncture meridians are the major power circuits for an infinite network of energy conductors that form the Body Electric. This Body Electric is responsible for producing your aura, the colorful glow of life that a psychic can see and that Kirlian photography can photograph. Science is just beginning to understand what metaphysicians (and Asian physicians) have known for ages, that our life force is not just inside our bodies, but surrounds us as long as life exists.

Because this Body Electric has both physical properties and spiritual properties, it allows an energy interchange to take place, so that physical experiences like the bath can affect your spirit in a profound way.

Although Western science has been slow to see the connection between body, mind, and spirit, many older and wiser cultures have understood this connection for millennia. The Chinese, Hindu, and Native American cultures all know that one cannot be healthy unless all three segments of the self—body, mind, and spirit—are in harmony.

The metaphysical bathing rituals in this book are

culled from many sources. They are offered to help you use this universal means of replenishment to heal, renew, and protect that most mysterious part of your being . . . your spirit. And, in turn, to bring your physical and metaphysical being into harmonious and fulfulling balance.

OVERVIEW OF

Metaphysical Baths

Yogi's Aura-Cleanse Bath

- Giving your energy field a good scrub.

Psychic-Healing Bath

- When you're feeling physically drained by someone.

Psychic-Protection Bath

- When you are under psychic attack.

Psychic-Awareness Bath

- Awakening your inner vision.

Heart/Mind-Connection Bath

- Removing blocks to success.

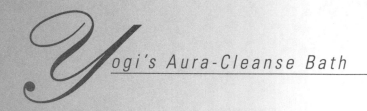

ogi's Aura-Cleanse Bath

PURPOSE   On the body level, this bath is superb for chemical detox, as well as for cleansing from radiation exposure, flu, colds, or other pathogenic invasions. This is the bath you take the *moment* you think you're getting sick!

On the spiritual side, this bath will cleanse negativity from your aura and leave your spirit clean, vital, and wonderfully refreshed.

1 lb. baking soda
½ lb. salt (sea salt is best, but table salt or kosher salt will do.)

OPTIONAL
Candles (bayberry or myrrh)
Harp music

HOW TO   To remove toxic chemicals from your body—be they drugs, alcohol, medicines, pesticides, radiation, or other environmental pollution—it is necessary to repeat this cleansing bath daily for seven consecutive days.

Fill the tub with comfortably warm water, add salt and soda. Soak for twenty minutes.

If at any time you begin to feel ill—nauseous, dizzy, or debilitated—leave the bath immediately, as it will have done its work of shaking loose the toxins in your system.

You will begin to feel lighter. If you have an awareness of your energy body, you will soon sense the increased movement within you.

To cleanse your Aura:

Soak in this salt/soda mixture as long as you wish. Allow yourself to sink into a gentle meditative state, letting your mind float outward with the buoyancy of water. Imagine your auric field interacting with the bath . . . picture the negative influences that have drained you being drawn out and washed away. Visualize anger, sorrow, uncertainty dissolving into the soothing water . . . see the psychic debris you have picked up from those around you dissipated from your energy field by the magnetism of the water.

Hints:

Harp music will set up a special resonance with your spirit, while the taped sound of Tibetan bells can initiate cleansing of its own. The light of candles will help to focus your attention on the Infinite. If scented with bayberry or myrrh, the added dimension of this incense will increase your awareness of spirit, without disturbing the meditative quality of your reverie. Afterward, try sleeping on a pillow filled with boxwood. Your shimmering aura may bring dreams of surprising clarity or precognition.

Psychic-Healing Bath

WHEN YOU'RE FEELING PSYCHICALLY DRAINED BY SOMEONE

PURPOSE   I call them Psychic Vampires—the people who seem capable of draining our vitality and life force. Sometimes they appear to do it on purpose, other times they are simply so depleted of energy themselves that they drain our batteries without even meaning to.

When you have been with such a person, be it a family member, coworker, friend, or lover, there is a simple bath that can replenish you and recharge your psychic batteries.

1 cup apple cider vinegar

HOW TO   Fill the tub with warmish water, add the vinegar, and soak for twenty minutes. Afterward, if you can, go outdoors barefoot, even if it is just for a few seconds, to ground the negativity you've been in contact with from your body. Imagine the negativity flowing out of you . . . through your feet, down, down into the benevolent bosom of Mother Earth, where she will purify and transform it into useful energy again.

Do not go to bed for at least an hour after this bath. Your body needs to rebalance itself, so just relax and treat yourself to some pleasurable activity, like reading or listening to music. You need to refill your reservoir, and remind yourself of your own worth as a child of the universe.

Often we are tempted to let needy people drain us, but that is not as the universe intended. Each of us is sacred, and has an obligation to protect and preserve both body and spirit.

Psychic-Protection Bath
WHEN YOU ARE UNDER PSYCHIC ATTACK

PURPOSE   There are times in life when we are besieged by the evil intention of others. The attacking force may be a thought form created by someone who means us ill. It may be a disembodied entity, an uneasy soul having difficulty making the transition into what we call "death." It may even be the directed evil intent of an enemy.

Whatever the cause of the attack, there is a Native American remedy that will repel such invasion and keep you safe.

5 drops cedar oil
4 drops myrrh oil can be added morning and night to the corners of the room you feel the most vulnerable in, to protect you from negative energy

O P T I O N A L
cedar chips to burn

HOW TO   Put 10 drops of pure (not synthetic) cedar oil into a warm tub and soak for twenty minutes. You may also wish to burn cedar chips in the vicinity of the bath, as the Indians do, to purify the environment.

Be sure to leave a window or a door open so that the "Spirit" energy has a means to escape.

120

A F F I R M A T I O N

There is a powerful prayer of protection you might also wish to use under these circumstances. Allow yourself to slip into a meditative mindset, a prayerful state of mind. If you know the identity of the attacking entity, use his or her name; if not, it won't matter, the prayer will work anyway. It goes like this:

By the power of Jesus Christ (or whichever deity or Universal Truth has most meaning for you) and with the intercession of my Angel Guardian, I command that you [name] leave my auric field. Return to your source and be lifted up for Light.

Say this aloud in a commanding tone until you feel the danger has passed.

You might want to add my favorite prayer of protection. This is a powerful protector, which I say many times a day. It came to me originally from Isabel Hickey, the great astrologer and metaphysician:

I clothe myself in a Robe of Light that is the Love and Power and Wisdom of God. Not only that I may be protected, but that anyone who comes in contact with me or sees me may be drawn to God and healed.

Envision yourself clothed in this splendid robe of light as you say the prayer, and you will be surprised at the powerful protective forces you will feel surrounding you.

Psychic-Awareness Bath
AWAKENING YOUR INNER VISION

PURPOSE   Encourages spiritual awareness and develops psychic faculties.

Mix 3 or more of this selection of oils in your bath, using 5 drops of each:

Lilac Oil—Helps to see past lives, induces clairvoyant powers.

Lemongrass—Aids psychic powers. Put some on your forehead also while bathing, as it is used by the mediums and spiritualists to make contact with the spirits.

Mimosa—For nighttime baths, it unlocks the door to your psychic mind. Keep a pad and pencil next to your bed and write down your dreams. Don't be surprised to find glimpses of the future in your dreams.

Juniper—For psychic protection and purification. Add to each psychic awareness bath.

Magnolia—Excellent for meditation and psychic development, peace and harmony.

Nutmeg—Promotes visions and expands consciousness. Just use a little!

Candle

Mix these gently into your warm tub, while you are in the water. Swirl the essences around your body.

The third eye is located in the center of your forehead, between your eyebrows. The mystics believe that by concentrating on this point, you will awaken your inner vision. If you practice the following exercise daily, you will definitely *feel* and experience your third eye.

While in this bath, you can practice this third-eye opening exercise. Here's how it works:

Burn a candle where you can see it. Stare into the flame, relaxing your eyes, and imagine the reflection of the candle flame at the center, between your eyebrows. Concentrate there for a minute or two, then repeat the process. After a while, just close your eyes, with your attention fixed on your third eye, and let yourself drift, but try to limit your thoughts as you do so. If your thoughts are overwhelming, try to stop your mind by concentrating on your breathing. If you count up to seven on each inhaled breath, and seven for each exhale, you will calm your mind, allowing your third eye to open.

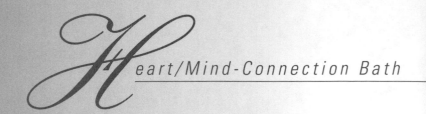

Heart/Mind-Connection Bath

PURPOSE   This bath helps you to remove any blocks you have to achieving the success you desire. Lavender releases emotional conflicts blocking spiritual growth, while lemon promotes mental clarity.

10 drops lavender oil
10 drops lemon oil

HOW TO   This bath should be taken in the morning to get the full benefit of its clearing energies. If you're nervous about exams or a business presentation, this is the perfect bath to prepare you.

As you are bathing, visualize the actual blocks being loosened from around your heart and solar plexus area. As they loosen, swish the water around you and feel them dissolve. When you get up from the bath, quickly rinse yourself with warm water to psychically cleanse the "blocks" from your body. Feel them go whirling down the drain and out of your life.

Releasing Blocks to Achieving Success:
This block comes from a lack of joy. If we have free-flowing joy we are able to accomplish anything. Look at the pure joy that a child embodies. A child doesn't

perceive any barriers or any obstacles, but runs free. Invoke this sense of freedom into every cell of your being while you are soaking in the bath. A child doesn't think and analyze every action—he or she just goes, flowing with ideas and the creativity inside that needs to be expressed. What is the barrier that prevents you from following through on your own creativity? Joy knows no boundaries.

A F F I R M A T I O N

Your affirmation should be:

My joy knows no boundaries.
I am totally free, and I
achieve fulfillment and success
in all aspects of my life.

Shopping List for Metaphysical Baths

GROCERY STORE

Apple cider vinegar
Baking soda
Salt, kosher or sea salt

ESSENTIAL OILS

Cedar oil
Frankincense
Juniper oil
Lavender oil
Lemon oil
Lemongrass oil
Lilac oil
Magnolia oil
Mimosa oil
Myrrh oil
Nutmeg oil

HEALTH FOOD STORE

Candles (Bayberry or Myrrh)
Cedar Chips

MUSIC:

Harp or Tibetan Bells

Part V

Beauty Baths

# Beauty and the Bath

Is beauty a quality of the face and body, or perhaps of the spirit? If all three play a part, what better place of enhancement could you find than the bathtub?

Cleopatra bathed in rose petals before seducing Mark Antony. Diane de Poitiers, who graced the bed of two kings, father and son, thought rainwater the only water pure enough to bathe her skin. The Sultan of Baghdad dispatched slaves to Cathay to bring back bathing oils to anoint the beauties of his seraglio, and it is said that his favorite, Kadin, attributed her rise in power to the bath oil she had the court magician concoct from the fragrance of night-blooming jasmine. Catherine the Great used vodka to cleanse her skin; it acts as a perfect astringent, taking off surface dirt to leave the skin glowing. Beware, you might get funny looks from your friends when they find the bottle of vodka in your bathroom medicine chest.

Because the bath is the one moment of tranquillity in our busy lives, it is the perfect time to concentrate on the fine art of being beautiful. There are centuries of beauty magic at our disposal, so we will divide this section into two distinct but harmonious categories: specific baths that are beautifying in themselves, and individual beauty treatments one can use while languorously lounging in the soothing waters.

Love-and-Beauty Meditation

As you lie in the tub, become aware of the beautiful fragrances permeating your aura from the perfumed oils. Close your eyes—inhale the fragrance, exhale your fatigue. Inhale again more deeply, and as you breathe out, allow all negativity to drain from your body and mind.

This is a time for letting go. Imagine yourself becoming empty—your mind as quiet as a tranquil woodland pool.

Become aware of your true essence. You are all alone. You are allowed to indulge your forces. You are free to experience pleasure. Imagine that this freedom gives you the magic power to create anything you want.

Feel the love in your heart—experience your soul resting there. This is your true identity—your true reality of pure love and pure beauty.

Let the love bubble up inside of you—let it flow to every cell of your body. Let it overflow into your mind and emotions.

You are drifting now to a new place of complete peace and contentment. There is nothing else—only your contemplation of self. You are perfect. You are the manifestation of the wondrous miracle of life.

Beauty Baths

Youthful-Glow Bath
- For maintaining or creating beautiful skin.

Soft-Touch Bath
- For the world's softest, youngest-looking skin.

Japanese Saki Bath for Radiant Beauty
- Make your skin glow.

Problem-Skin Bath
- Dryness, oiliness, irritation, inflammation, and acne.

Supple-Skin Bath
- Create ageless, smoother, tighter skin.

All-Over Sea-Smoother Bath
- Polish your body.

Air-Quality-Control Bath
- Rejuvenating yeast mask.

Edible Beauty-Mask Bath
- Breakfast for the skin.

Natural Face-Lifts for the Bath
- Don't confuse these with lunch!

Healing-Capillaries Bath
- Erase the map on your face.

Healing-Sunburn Bath
- Take the heat out of your skin.

Youthful-Glow Bath
FOR MAINTAINING OR CREATING BEAUTIFUL SKIN

PURPOSE   There is no reason not to have beautiful skin well into old age. The youthful glow has nothing to do with physical age; it has to do with the energy within. This youthful skin bath is a long-term project. Make it part of your weekly beauty regime and your skin will always glow, at every age.

There are many women who maintained their beauty well into their eighties. Gloria Swanson and Cleopatra are two famous women who maintained their youthful beauty well into their mature years, as did Helen of Troy, who at fifty looked twenty. Perhaps their secrets for youthful skin have to do with this ancient, but still extremely popular, oil bath.

4 drops sesame oil
3 drops avocado oil
2 drops almond oil
(Use cold-pressed oils)

HOW TO   You can combine these oils ahead of time and keep them in a well-sealed bottle at room temperature. When you're ready for your bath, pour in several drops. This combination is one of the most beautifying known. For extra pleasure, add your favorite essential oil to this bath. Then close your eyes and let yourself drift into loveliness.

This combination of oils is also excellent for removing makeup, and may also be used every day as a complexion enhancer.

Soft-Touch Bath
FOR THE WORLD'S SOFTEST, YOUNGEST-
LOOKING SKIN

PURPOSE   I have been doing this bath for fifteen years, and children always comment on how wonderfully soft my skin is. A child I'm close to says I have the softest skin he's ever felt, and a male acquaintance of mine always asks if he might touch my hand or my arm, because he loves the softness. It has become a joke among our circle of friends, because he might be having dinner with a date in a restaurant, and still stop by to ask to touch my skin.

1 tsp. (or more) coconut oil

OPTIONAL
your favorite essential oil

HOW TO   Coconut oil is my secret. It comes in a jar and looks a bit like Crisco. Sometimes I melt the coconut oil under the sun, or hot running water, and then add a few drops of rose oil before letting it harden again. That way there is always a beautiful scent in the bath.

Another option is to leave the coconut oil unscented, and have on hand some favorite essential oils. Just add the fragrance you desire (or are most in need of).

Here are some suggestions for essential oils:

Rose—for spring fever, for the heart, or to ease depression

Sandalwood—to calm the nervous system

Rosemary—for all-around rejuvenation

This bath does not work well with cedar oil, because that oil releases negative energy, and the dissipation of that energy can be impeded by the density of the coconut oil.

Japanese Saki Bath
for Radiant Beauty
MAKE YOUR SKIN GLOW

Bathing in rice wine (saki) is a three thousand-year-old tradition in Japan. The fame of saki's ability to enhance beauty is legendary. Just ask any geisha. Their skin is famous for softness, clarity, and radiance.

2 qts. saki (or 1.8 liter bottle)

This is an expensive but wonderful bath. Take a shower first to cleanse yourself, then pour the saki into a hot tub and relax for thirty minutes. You'll be amazed how radiant and soft your skin will look and feel. (Also, at how dirty the bath water becomes, because saki is excellent at drawing toxins from the body.) Take this bath when you want to feel more beautiful and have the desire to indulge yourself with decadence that actually benefits you.

Problem-Skin Baths
DRYNESS, OILINESS, IRRITATION, INFLAMMATION, AND ACNE

PURPOSE Certain essential oils work for specific skin problems. Some days your skin may feel itchy, other days just dry or irritated. The basic bath principles are the same, so I'll give you the solution and you can match it up to your problem.

These special baths work best when the ingredients are mixed beforehand and stored in airtight containers in a cool, dark place. Each bath uses essential oils mixed with your choice of a cold-pressed pure vegetable oil or, in some cases, jojoba oil. You can figure two tablespoons of oil per bath, while the amount of drops of essential oils (see ingredients section) are for a small container (small jelly-jar size). In all cases, shake the oils together with the vegetable oil, to blend their fragrances—and their special powers!

DRY SKIN:
7 drops sandalwood oil
5 drops geranium oil
5 drops ylang-ylang oil
3 drops rosewood oil

OILY SKIN:
10 drops lemon oil
8 drops cypress or camphor oil
5 drops lavender oil
Mix this with jojoba oil.

IRRITATED OR INFLAMED SKIN:
8 drops sandalwood oil
4 drops blue chamomile oil
4 drops rose oil
Mix this with jojoba oil.

ACNE:
20 drops Bergamot oil
5 drops juniper oil
4 drops cypress or 15 drops tea tree oil
Mix this with jojoba oil.

After each bath, clean the tub thoroughly, to wash   HOW TO
away the excess oils—as well as the unwanted energy.

143

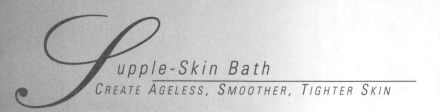

Supple-Skin Bath
CREATE AGELESS, SMOOTHER, TIGHTER SKIN

PURPOSE   This bath, combined with its face mask, relaxes the body while allowing your skin to release its own natural glow.

FACIAL
1 cup fresh cucumber juice
1/4 cup honey

BATH
8 drops jasmine oil
8 drops fennel oil

HOW TO   This is one of the best ways of keeping your skin youthful and supple. Mix the cucumber juice and honey, then apply it to your face and neck using cotton balls. Apply it in upward strokes starting at the base of your neck and stroking gently toward your forehead. Avoid the eye area. Leave this mixture on, and immerse yourself in a hot bath with jasmine and fennel oil essence. This will tighten your skin, while replenishing its essential oil content.

Don't forget to unplug your phone and put up the DO NOT DISTURB sign on the bathroom door. This is a great time to listen to soothing music and allow yourself to feel the music penetrating your heart, mind, and soul, while the bath ingredients improve your skin.

All-Over Sea-Smoother Bath

This bath removes the dry flakes and scales from your moisture-deprived skin. It is equally good for cold or warm climates. If your skin is dry and flaky, this bath is a "must try."

Epsom salts—1 lb.
½ cup cold-pressed sunflower oil (or olive, or peanut)

Mix the salt and oil together, and, starting at your toes, massage your body with small portions of the mix so you feel the scrubbing effect of the salt on your skin. If the salt melts too quickly in the hot bath, do the salt/oil scrub first and then relax in the tub to let the oil refresh your skin.

This one will really get you glowing!

Air-Quality-Control Bath
REJUVENATING YEAST MASK

PURPOSE   Because of the stress and pollution in our lives and environment, it is important to take time to properly reoxygenate and cleanse the skin. Used once a month, this mask will help counteract the aging effects of environmental pollution. This is excellent for city dwellers or people who spend a lot of time in airplanes or in their cars.

2 tbsp. powdered brewer's yeast
3 tbsp. warm water
5 drops lavender oil
5 drops Roman chamomile oil

HOW TO   Mix the yeast with the water until it's gravy smooth. Apply it to your face and neck in upward strokes with your fingertips. Leave it on for fifteen to thirty minutes while you soak in your favorite relaxing bath with lavender and Roman chamomile essential oils.

Edible Beauty-Mask Bath
BREAKFAST FOR THE SKIN

This mask helps to restore a youthful glow to your face. That bright, shiny face you had as a child will reemerge after this special mask. **PURPOSE**

8 oz. of oatmeal
1 drop rose essence
A few drops of almond oil (soya can be substituted, always cold-pressed)
Gauze

Mix together the oatmeal, rose essence, and almond oil into a paste and spread it on the gauze. Fold a clean piece of gauze over the mixture and apply it to each side of your face. Do another section for your forehead, and one for your neck. **HOW TO**

Then just relax in a warm tub for a quarter hour. After fifteen minutes, you can remove the gauze pads and gently scrub your entire body with the paste. Rinse off with a quick, warm shower, and your skin will glow all day!

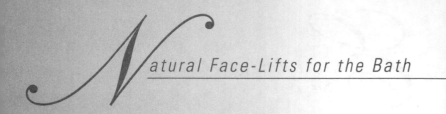

Natural Face-Lifts for the Bath

PURPOSE   These natural face-lifts can be used in conjunction with any of the baths in this book.

Relaxing in the bath is a great time for a face-lift. There's no need to talk, which means those laughter and frown lines get a much-needed rest.

MASK ONE—ANTI-POLLUTION MASK
2 tsp. clay
2 tsp. oatmeal
2 tsp. honey

MASK TWO—SOFT SKIN MASK
1 cup yogurt
2 tsp. honey

MASK THREE—REJUVENATING TIRED SKIN MASK OR
  "WAKE UP THE SKIN"
2 tsp. wheat germ oil
2 tsp. lemon juice
2 tsp. clay

Mix this gooey paste together and let it sit while you fill your tub. Put all your hair carefully off your face with a headband and shower cap. Blend the paste onto your face in upward strokes starting at the base of your neck and moving up to your forehead. Be sure to avoid your eyes!

Relax in the bath for fifteen to twenty minutes and think pleasant thoughts. Relive in memory the most wonderful moments in your life. When you're ready to remove the mask, rinse it off in the sink with lukewarm water.

ealing-Capillaries Bath
ERASE THE MAP ON YOUR FACE

PURPOSE   This bath and mask are designed to help heal the tiny broken blood vessels on your face.

3 drops each of essential oils of:
Mint
Bay
Laurel
Rosemary

HOW TO   Mix the oils together and after tying back your hair, massage the formula into your face and other affected areas. Then, immerse yourself in a tub filled with your favorite aromatic scent, and relax thoroughly. After fifteen to twenty minutes, rinse off the mixture with warm water.

Healing-Sunburn Bath

PURPOSE   We all know how damaging the sun is to our delicate
skin tissue. Sometimes, in the overwhelming joy of ex-
periencing sun after a long, cold winter, we forget the
need to protect ourselves and we get the traditional
(and dangerous) sunburn. Don't worry. Help is only a
bathtub away.

This bath helps heal skin burned by the sun.

5 drops each of essential oils of:
Peppermint
Lavender
Roman chamomile
Fresh lemon

HOW TO   Mix the oils together and in a lukewarm bath. Relax
and let the oils coat your sensitive skin.

If you are just using fresh lemons, rub the cut fresh
lemon on your burned skin. This will sting! But it will
also help heal you. If it's too uncomfortable, dilute the
lemon slightly with water.

If you are on vacation, you can use the same substances in tea bag form and lie in a tea bath made up of
peppermint, chamomile, and lemon tea (or real
lemons).

Shopping List for Beauty Baths

Cold-Pressed Oils
Almond oil
Avocado oil
Coconut oil
Jojoba oil
Olive oil
Sesame oil
Sunflower oil
Wheat Germ oil

Grocery Store
Brewer's Yeast
Chamomile tea
Cucumbers
Epsom salts—1 lb. per bath
Honey
Lemons
Oatmeal
Peppermint tea
Yogurt—plain/no sugar

Essential Oils
Bay
Bergamot
Blue chamomile
Camphor
Cypress
Fennel
Geranium
Jasmine
Juniper
Laurel
Lavender
Lemon
Mint
Orange
Peppermint
Roman chamomile
Rose
Rosemary
Rosewood
Sandalwood
Ylang-ylang

Part VI

Pleasure and Sexuality Baths

*T*he Pleasure Bath

Showering with a friend may save water, but *bathing* with one elevates pleasure to a whole new dimension.

The bath gives you a sensual, self-indulgent, *private* time for you and the one you love to explore each other's pleasure parameters. Take time out from the constant drumming of life's everyday demands to pay attention to each other's needs and desires.

Why not set aside one evening a week for pure, unadulterated pleasure? Put the kiddies (or animals) to bed, turn on the stereo, turn down the lights, and fill the bathroom with candles instead of electric lights. You're going to create an altogether different kind of electricity.

Wax creative. If it suddenly seems a good idea to scatter rose petals in the water, do it. Two glasses of champagne or sparkling cider at the side of the tub can make the candlelight all the more romantic.

Whatever your pleasure, this is the time. Intimacy will take on a whole new meaning if you give the special pleasure baths in this chapter a chance to transport both of you to your own private paradise.

Pleasure and Sexuality Baths

Sexual-Vitality Bath

- To release your inhibitions.

Mystical-Sex Bath

- Bringing you a night of romantic and sensual pleasure.

Wake-Up-Your-Sex-Life Bath

- Revitalize passions that have waned.

The Erotic Bath

- When you need added inspiration.

Rose Bath

- For those couples wanting to conceive a child.

Playful Baths with a Partner

- Fun, erotic delight.

Sexual-Rejuvenation Bath

- To revive your mate's sexual desire.

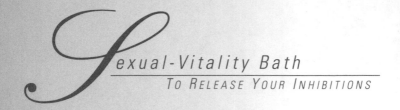

Sexual-Vitality Bath
To Release Your Inhibitions

PURPOSE

This bath can help to strengthen the male organ and can also help with frigidity.

5 drops jasmine oil
5 drops sandalwood oil
Sexy music, candles, flowers

HOW TO

Before making love, take a bath with your partner. These bath oils are known to be aphrodisiacs. Sandalwood helps one to relax, and jasmine stimulates desire.

Choose some romantic, sexy music and combine it with candles and even some fresh flowers. Turn off the lights. Relate all the amusing things that happened during the day or, if that's not possible, tell each other jokes. Avoid talking about the problems of the day or any intellectual discussions. If you like, massage each other's shoulders and/or feet—especially around the ankles and heels where you'll find the sexual reflex points. Then relax in each other's arms, and let the room and the oils work their magic!

ystical-Sex Bath
BRINGING YOU A NIGHT OF
ROMANTIC AND SENSUAL PLEASURE

PURPOSE   Let your spirit soar with your partner, with this powerful combination of aphrodisiac oils. This will be sure to bring you a night of romantic and sensual pleasures. Turn off your phone and lock your door!!!

3 drops rose oil (Used to open the heart. Rose oil gets the emotions flowing, which puts you in the mood for romance)
3 drops jasmine (Jasmine stimulates the sexual appetite)
3 drops sandalwood (This relaxes the nervous system while awakening desire)
3 drops frankincense (Used in rituals to promote dreams)
3 drops ylang-ylang (This has very strong aphrodisiac properties)

Luscious chocolate (Montezuma always drank a cup of chocolate before entering his harem)
Champagne or hot chocolate (Both proven aphrodisiacs)

Romantic music (Suggestions: Chopin's piano waltzes, or Harry Nilsson's A Little Touch of Schmilsson in the Night)
Bouquet of fragrant pink or red roses

After adjusting the temperature of the bath water so that it is *mutually* comfortable, make sure the music is on, the flowers are in view, the door is locked, and the phone is turned off. Add the combination of the oils, swirling them around in the water with your hand.

How to

Get in, and let the magic happen!

Wake-Up-Your-Sex-Life Bath
REVITALIZE PASSIONS THAT HAVE WANED

PURPOSE   To revive and renew the passion and love in your life.

3 drops magnolia oil
5 drops nutmeg oil
5 drops Arabian musk oil

Great champagne or a sparkling cider
A tray of special hors d'oeuvres (finger food) to feed each other in the tub

Lots of candles, scented with your favorite scents

Your favorite romantic music, such as Debussy's La Mer

HOW TO   Look great when your lover walks in the door wearing what you know is a turn-on . . . fantasy clothing that you feel sexy wearing. Create a romantic setting in the bathroom and bedroom using lots of candles, and sheets lightly scented with an aphrodisiac oil (in the corners, where it won't stain).

Bring the hors d'oeuvres and champagne (or sparkling cider) into the bathroom and start the music.

Once in the tub begin by recalling the most romantic moments of your lives together. Fantasize together about traveling to exotic places, and reawakening your passions there.

Make sure that your hum-drum chores are out of the way so you can totally relax and let the evening develop sensuously. No talking business, kids, or problems.

The Erotic Bath
WHEN YOU NEED ADDED INSPIRATION

PURPOSE   Sometimes inspiration has to come from sources other than your mate. This bath is a true turn-on!

4 drops pure sandalwood oil
4 drops ginger oil
4 drops rose oil (optional)

Sandalwood is the most powerful aphrodisiac. It calms the nervous system and melts away the tensions and inhibitions that prevent us from letting go sexually and emotionally. Sandalwood has been used as a perfume in the Near and Far East and in Europe for longer than recorded history.

HOW TO   Take this bath alone or with a partner. If you need added stimulation, use fantasy or erotic literature. You can read the stories by Anaïs Nin to each other, or other appropriate books or magazines. Remember, fantasy is more important than mental anxiety over whether you will be able to reach an orgasm. Feel the oils seep into your pores and all the responsive areas of your body, and just let yourself go to wherever the aphrodisiac bath chooses to take you.

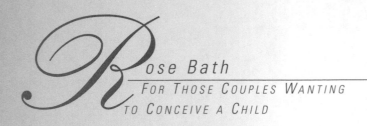

Rose Bath

For Those Couples Wanting to Conceive a Child

PURPOSE   A child can be the ultimate expression of a couple's love. If you're having difficulty conceiving, this bath can help increase the sperm count in men. Don't make the water scalding hot.

10 drops of rose oil

OPTIONAL
A few handfuls of rose petals or bouquet of roses

How to   When trying to conceive, take a bath together before making love.

You might also want to explore this special love meditation for conception.

Before making love, sit together and synchronize your breathing—inhale and exhale together. Close your eyes and mentally invite a special soul to enter your lives. Tell it of the love you will give it, and the joy this soul will add to your lives. Tell the soul you want its vibration to be in harmony with you and with your family. You want the *right* soul to enter through your lovemaking, to be part of your family forever. Imagine these mental vibrations traveling into the universe, and invoke the angels for their assistance in helping you conceive the perfect child for you. (At the end of your meditation, don't forget to thank the angels for their help.)

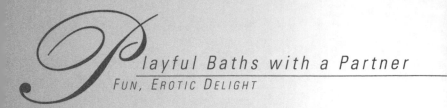

PURPOSE   Never underestimate the power of massage. There are reflex points all over your body that can be stimulated for wonderful results. We know we are at our best sexually when our minds are least cluttered, so why not use the bath massage as a means of purging mental tensions from our bodies and making room for pleasurable results?

5 drops ylang-ylang oil
10 drops rose oil
5 drops patchouli oil

HOW TO   Both of you relax in the warm tub and add the oils.
Start by gently stroking your partner's shoulder and arms, down to the fingertips, then repeat on the other arm. Now take each hand, one at a time, and with your thumbs on the inside of the palms, press as if you are kneading bread. The fatty area on the lower part of the palms under the thumb (known as the Mound of Venus) is especially important. Repeat on legs and feet, then proceed to the shoulders again. By now, your partner should be drifting happily into your unhurried caresses. You might want to consider any good massage book or tape to provide new possibilities.

ANOTHER OPTION:

Buy a set of bath paints and paint each other's bodies . . . light the bathroom with a dozen candles . . . let your imagination be your only limitation. Throw caution to the winds and think of the bath as a sensuous preamble to other pleasures.

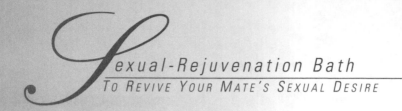

Sexual-Rejuvenation Bath
TO REVIVE YOUR MATE'S SEXUAL DESIRE

PURPOSE   If your partner occasionally has a problem respond-
            ing to you sexually, here is a way to get things going.

            4 drops sandalwood oil
            4 drops vanilla oil
            4 drops ylang-ylang oil
            4 drops ginger oil

HOW TO   Invite your partner to take a relaxing bath with you
            and offer him a massage. The main areas to focus on
            during the massage are the head and neck. There are
            reflex points on the top of the head toward the hairline
            that are specific for toning the male organ. Just apply
            pressure to the top of the entire head with your
            thumbs. You can do this while cradling his head in
            your chest. Then go to his neck and massage the kinks
            out of it. Next go to his feet. Using the pressure of the
            thumbs of both hands, drain the stress from the soles
            of his feet. Then concentrate next on the area around
            the ankles and heels. Strong (but not uncomfortable)
            pressure is recommended. These points stimulate the
            sexual organs.

When you've got him back in the bedroom, massage the lower back, especially around the coccyx area. You don't need much pressure; apply it as he likes.

Some men respond immediately, or sometimes it takes a day or so, but many of my clients have been quite pleased with the results!

Shopping List for Pleasure and Sexuality Baths

Essential Oils

Arabian musk	Nutmeg
Cedar	Patchouli
Frankincense	Rose
Ginger	Rose petals
Jasmine	Sandalwood
Magnolia	Ylang-ylang

Specialty Store

Candles	Chocolates
Champagne, Sparkling	Roses
Cider	

Music

Chopin's piano waltzes	Your choice
Debussy's *La Mer*	

Part VII

Crystal Baths

A Cherokee Legend
(ABOUT CRYSTALS)

AS TOLD BY KENNETH COHEN IN
"BONES OF OUR ANCESTORS"

Yoga Journal, February 1985

In ancient times human beings lived in harmony with Nature. They spoke the same language as the animals. They hunted, fished, and foraged only to satisfy their needs, always offering a prayer of thanks when they had to take life. According to the Hopis, the spot on the crown of the head, the fontanel, remained soft throughout life. Through this soft spot people received information from the Creator about where to live and how to live in balance. They retained the innocence and simplicity of childhood.

As time passed, people lost this innocence; the soft spot hardened. Some traditions claim this was the work of the Devil or, as the Jews say, the *yetzerhara,* the evil impulse locked in the human unconscious. Other believed this was just the natural course of events: human beings had to lose Oneness in order to regain it through their prayers of gratitude. They killed the animals and each other for sport or pleasure.

The Bear Tribe, chief among the animals, called a conference of all the animals. Something had to be done. The Bears suggested, "When the humans shoot their arrow at us, why don't we shoot back?" But the bow and arrow required too great a sacrifice. One bear had to give up his life so that his sinew could be used for the bowstring. And when the time came to actually shoot the bow, the bear's claws got stuck on the string. Obviously, this would never work.

So the deer offered another suggestion. "We will bring disease into the world. Each of us will be responsible for a different illness. When humans live out of balance with Nature, when they forget to give thanks for their food, they will get sick." And in fact the Deer invoked rheumatism and arthritis, and each animal invoked another disease.

But the Plant Tribe, always more sympathetic, felt that this was too harsh a punishment. So they volunteered: "For every disease a human gets, one of us will be present to cure their ailments and regain their balance." All of Nature agreed to this strategy. One plant, in particular, spoke out louder than the rest. This was Tobacco, the chief of the plants. He said "I will not cure any disease, but I will help people return to the sacred way of life, provided I am smoked or offered with prayers and ceremony. But, if I am misused, and merely smoked for pleasure, I will cause cancer, the worst disease of all."

The close friends of the Plant Tribe, the Rocks and Minerals, agreed to help the Plants. Each mineral would have a spiritual power, a subtle vibration that could be used to regain perfect health. The Ruby, if worn as an amulet, would heal the heart; the Emerald would heal the liver and the eyes, and so on. The chief of the mineral tribe, Quartz Crystal, was clear, like the light of Creation itself. Quartz put his arm around his brother Tobacco and said, "I will be the sacred mineral. I will heal the mind. I will help humans see the origin of the disease. I will help to bring wisdom and clarity in dreams. And I will record their spiritual history, including our meeting today, so that in the future, if humans gaze into me, *they* may *see* their origin and the way of harmony." And so it was, and is to this day.

Crystal Healing Baths

Crystals may or may not be all that the Cherokee legend suggests, but one thing we know for certain about them: crystals act as a kind of energy transmitter. The first radios were "crystal sets," and all modern television technology is based on the use of crystal microchips for transmission. Because various forms of crystals vibrate at varied frequencies, different gem stones affect the human body in different ways. For example, ruby is a blood purifier and heart strengthener, emerald affects the eyes and liver, amethyst impacts the spiritual centers, and so on.

If we think of our bodies as Chinese medicine does—as an intricate electrical network, constantly vibrating with *qi*, or life energy—it becomes easier to visualize the ways in which the vibrations of crystals might impact our health and vitality.

The following recipe for immortality from an ancient Taoist text is a charming indication of the confidence the Chinese placed in crystals.

Ancient Chinese Recipe for Immortality

1. *Take 5 pieces of clear quartz*
2. *Round and polish them in a whetstone*
3. *Cook the crystals in a mixture of shallots, honey, and ferns*
4. *After the mixture is cooled, ingest while invoking the Lords of the Five Directions*

Each crystal will enter one of the five major organs of the body: spleen, heart, kidneys, lungs, and liver—and preserve it from decay!

By the way, the Chinese glyph (letter) for quartz is *Shui Ching*, which translates as "water essence," the same word used in ancient times for the moon.

We know that the medicinal significance of water is nearly limitless, so imagine what happens when it is magnetized and empowered by the addition of crystals.

Since the beginning of time, gems and crystals have been coveted not only for their beauty and power, but for their medicinal properties. Indian shamans, Egyptian priests, and Greek gods and oracles have pronounced that crystals and gems endowed the power to heal, mesmerize, and conquer. The Atlanteans so perfected harnessing of crystal energy that it is believed they used precious and semiprecious gems and crystals to heal virtually every disease and ailment known to man.

If you begin to experiment with the healing powers of the crystals in your bathwater, you may be very pleasantly surprised with the power of your positive results. Remember, crystal transmits energy; bathwater amplifies that charge.

OVERVIEW OF

Crystal Baths

Citrine Crystal Success-and-Power Bath
- Empower yourself for success.

Quartz Crystal Healing-and-Energizing Bath
- Cleanse your aura and activate your body's healing power.

Rose Quartz Heart-Transforming Bath
- Heal your heart and open yourself to love.

Mystical-Dream Bath
- Let yourself be transported to the realm of magical dreams.

Amethyst Uplifting Spiritual Bath
- Connect with your Inner Vision and Higher Self.

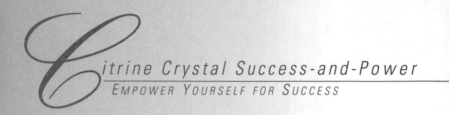

itrine Crystal Success-and-Power
EMPOWER YOURSELF FOR SUCCESS

PURPOSE Use this bath when you need to be empowered to achieve success, for example, to win a court case or to close a business deal.

One or more natural citrine quartz crystals

Cleanse the crystals before using, by soaking them in saltwater for at least fifteen minutes (2 tsp. salt to 8 oz. of water). I always say a prayer as I do this, asking the crystal angels to purify the stones and dedicate them to healing and good works.

HOW TO Before entering your tub, take a few minutes to clear your mind, and think about your specific goals. If you want, write them down, listing all aspects of the problem and the specific outcomes. *Be clear on your goals!*

Now, carefully place your citrine crystals into your tub full of water.

Once you are comfortable and relaxed, imagine yourself in the room where the meeting will take place, even if you have never been there before. Next, imagine the people involved. See yourself clearly in this environment. See your aura filled vibrantly with the yellow-golden energy of the citrine, empowering you and giving you acute mental clarity, enabling you to influence those involved in the meeting toward your way of thinking. Remember to do this with love and positive energy. Now, with confidence, visualize your goals achieved to everyone's mutual satisfaction. The next day, take the citrine crystal with you to the real meeting—to remind you of your intended success!

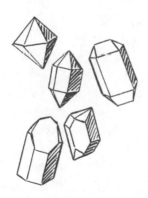

Quartz Crystal Healing-and Energizing Bath
CLEANSE YOUR AURA AND ACTIVATE YOUR BODY'S HEALING POWER

PURPOSE

Quartz crystals are powerful healers. They clean your aura and release blocked energy so that your body's healing power can do its work.

Quartz crystals (1 or more)

Cleanse the crystals before using, by soaking them in salt-water for at least fifteen minutes (2 tsp. salt to 8 oz. of water). I always say a prayer as I do this, asking the crystal angels to purify the stones and dedicate them to healing and good works.

HOW TO

Place one or more quartz crystals in your tub. If you have several, place them all around your tub.

While in the bath, concentrate on the area of your body that needs healing. Imagine the healing energy of the crystals being activated, and direct these rays of light to where they are needed. Use creative visualization to see the pain leaving your body, or your organs being regenerated, or whatever healing grace is needed. You can even visualize the crystal's rays breaking up a tumor.

Whatever your problem is, see the crystals' healing rays dissipating the pain, totally rejuvenating you, and bringing you back to a perfect state of balance and harmony!

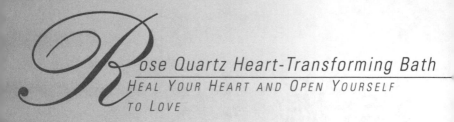

Rose Quartz Heart-Transforming Bath
HEAL YOUR HEART AND OPEN YOURSELF TO LOVE

PURPOSE   Rose quartz is a healer for the heart. It is calming and soothing, perfect for those times when you feel hurt, misunderstood, or betrayed. It opens us up to Divine Love, and helps us see things in a clearer, more compassionate way.

Rose quartz—one or more crystals

Cleanse the crystals before using, by soaking them in salt-water for at least fifteen minutes (2 tsp. salt to 8 oz. of water). I always say a prayer as I do this, asking the crystal angels to purify the stones and dedicate them to healing and good works.

OPTIONAL
Candles and incense

Place the rose quartz crystals in your tub. Light some candles and incense and, if you wish, play soothing music.

As you relax in the tub, become intensely aware of your breathing, following it in and out. Next move your concentration to your heartbeat for a few minutes. Try to imagine a beautiful pink light emanating from the rose quartz crystals and spiraling into your heart center. Let this pink light soothe your heartache. Imagine the pink light radiating from your heart and bathing your entire body with celestial love.

Let your anger and fear be melted by this love. Imagine the person or persons that have caused you pain, and see them surrounded by a pink bubble of light. Watch the differences between you melted by this love light. See yourselves forgiving each other and embracing.

Now imagine yourself floating in a pink sea of love, happy and fulfilled, in a state of perfect contentment.

Mystical-Dream Bath
LET YOURSELF BE TRANSPORTED TO THE REALM OF MAGICAL DREAMS

PURPOSE   Herkimer diamonds are a form of quartz crystal found in Herkimer, New York, and also in Brazil. They look like diamonds, and have many brilliant terminations, or facets.

Herkimer crystals are wonderful for releasing stress, both physically and emotionally. They also have the power to transport you to the higher realms of the spirit, and bring you to mystical consciousness in the dream state.

One or more Herkimer diamonds
Candles, incense, music

HOW TO   The best time to do this is in the evening before bedtime.

Gently place the diamonds into your bathtub. Put on some dreamy music; light some candles and incense. Then just let these crystals work their magic.

Soak in the tub for as long as you want, letting your mind drift wherever the Herkimers take it. When you finish your bath, rinse the crystals in cold water for a minute or two and then place them under your pillow. Enjoy pleasant dreams.

Make sure you go right to bed—no last-minute business calls, or other distractions.

Amethyst Uplifting Spiritual Bath

PURPOSE   The American Indians believe amethyst protects us
from evil spirits. The Greeks used amethyst as a cure
for drunkenness. They believed it would keep a man
safe, give him a clear mind, and open him up to higher
realms of mind and spirit.

Use this bath when you feel under psychic attack, or
are trying to break free from your addictions, or just
when you need a spiritual lift.

*Gather one or several amethyst stones that you've cleansed
by soaking them in saltwater for about fifteen minutes (2
tsp. salt to 8 oz. water).*

Candles

HOW TO   Place the amethyst crystals in your tub. Light some
candles—purple if you have them. And make sure
you'll be undisturbed.

Begin to relax by closing your eyes and concentrating on your breathing. Inhale and exhale deeply
twenty times. Now, place your attention on the flame
of a candle and look at it with relaxed, half-crossed
eyes. After a minute or two, close your eyes and try to

see the reflection of the candle in the "third eye" at the center of your forehead, between your eyebrows.

Repeat this exercise a few times, and then relax and close your eyes. Keep your mind on your third eye.

Since amethyst is a very powerful crystal, don't do this when you are in a mentally unstable state of mind, as it may agitate you and make you feel anxious.

Shopping List for Crystal Baths

Crystal Shop

Amethyst
Citrine
Herkimer diamonds
Quartz crystals
Rose quartz

Other

Candles
Music
Incense

General Shopping List
and Resource Guide

Many of the ingredients in this book can be found in your

local supermarket or health-food store. If, however, what

you are looking for is not available, sources have been

listed so that you may call or write to order what you can't

find locally.

ESSENTIAL OILS

Arabian Musk	Lily of the valley
Bay	Magnolia
Basil	Marjoram
Cedar	Mint
Chamomile	Nutmeg
Eucalyptus	Orange blossom
Fennel	Patchouli
Frankincense	Peppermint
Ginger	Rose
Grapefruit	Rosemary
Jasmine	Sage
Juniper	Sandalwood
Kyphi	Thyme
Laurel	Vanilla
Lavender	Violet
Lemon	Ylang-Ylang

Herb Store Supplies

Chamomile	Rosemary
Chaparral	Sage
Comfrey	Thyme
Ginger	Whole cloves

Health-Food Store Supplies

Almond oil
Avocado oil
Chamomile flowers and
tea bags
Coconut oil
Jojoba oil
Incense
Loofah sponge
Sea salt
Sesame oil
Vitamin C
Homeopathic remedies

Bach Flower Remedies
(can be ordered from
homeopathic suppliers—
see list beginning on the
following page)
Chestnut bud
Crab Apple
Rescue Remedy
Walnut

SUPERMARKET SUPPLIES

Apple cider vinegar
Baking soda
Epsom Salts
Honey
Kosher or sea salt
Powdered ginger

SPECIALTY SHOP SUPPLIES

Aztec Secret
French freeze-dried seaweed

Acupuncture chart
Hand reflexology chart

HOMEOPATHIC REMEDIES

BOERICK & TAFEL, INC.
1011 Arch Street
Philadelphia, PA 19107

BOIRON
6 Campus Boulevard, Building A
Newtown Square, PA 17073
1-800-258-8823

DOLISOS
6125 W. Tropicana Avenue
Las Vegas, NV 89102
702-871-7153

FOUNDATION FOR HOMEOPATHIC EDUCATION & RESEARCH
2124 Kittridge Street
Berkeley, CA 94704
510-649-8930

EHRHART, KARL
17 North Wabash Avenue
Chicago, IL 60602

D. L. THOMPSON
Homeopathic Supplies
844 Yonge Street
Toronto, 5 ONT CANADA M4W 2H1

MICKEY'S CHEMIST
88 2nd Avenue
NY, NY 10017
212-223-6333

BACH FLOWER REMEDIES

ELLON BACH USA, INC.
644 Merrick Road
Lynbrook, NY 11563-9815
516-593-2206

HERBS

APHRODESIA
282 Bleecker Street
New York, NY 10018

ATTAR HERBS AND SPICES
Playground Road
New Ipswitch, NH 03071
603-878-1780 ($50 min.)

EYE OF THE CAT
3314 East Broadway
Long Beach, CA 90803

FRONTIER COOPERATIVE HERBS
Box 299
Norway, IA
1-800-786-1388
($100 min.)

G'S HERBS, INC.
2344 NW 21st Place
Portland, OR 97210
503-241-1131

HEALTH CENTER FOR BETTER LIVING
6189 Taylor Road
Naples, FL 33942
813-566-2611

INDIANA BOTANIC GARDENS, INC.
626 177th Street
P.O. Box 5
Hammond, IN 46325
219-947-4040

NATURAL PRODUCTS SUPPLY CO.
24 East Bund Street
Shippenberg, PA 17257
717-532-2566

ESSENTIAL OILS

AROMA VERA INC.
P.O. Box 3609
Culver City, CA 90231

D'NAMIS LTD.
P.O. Box 672
Northport, NY 11768
516-754-3535

FLEUR
8 Bador Road
London, England N8

KIEHL'S PHARMACY
109 3rd Avenue
New York, NY 10003
212-475-3400

LOTUS LIGHT
P.O. Box 2
Wilmot, WI 53192
414-862-2395 or 1-800-548-3824

PEGASUS PRODUCTS
PO Box 228
Boulder, CO 80306
800-527-6104
(*Also CRYSTAL TINCTURES)

SANTA FE FRAGRANCE
PO Box 482
Santa Fe, NM 87504
505-473-1717

DEAD SEA SALTS

JERICHO FROM THE DEAD SEA
849 South Broadway
Suite 452
Los Angeles, CA 90014
213-891-9440

FRENCH FREEZE-DRIED SEAWEED

PHYTOMER
3350 South Highland Drive
Salt Lake City, UT 84106
800-227-8051

(Phytomer has offices in England, Canada, Japan and France)

70 Rue du Commandant l'Herminier
B.P. 40-35404 Saint-Malo Cedex (France)
Tel. 99.40.24.69 (add 011-Country Code + #)

CRYSTALS

MARY MURYN
111 Cross Highway
Westport, CT 06880
203-454-1994

For the Tubside Shopper

To make your bathing ritual odyssey a little bit easier, I've assembled some starter kits that encompass the basic ingredients needed for each section of this book.

THE BATH STARTER KITS:

- Emotional Soothing Baths Starter Kit
- Homeopathic Baths Starter Kit
- Healing Baths Starter Kit
- Metaphysical Baths Starter Kit
- Beauty Baths Starter Kit
- Pleasure and Sexuality Baths Starter Kit
- Crystal Baths Starter Kit

Specialty Kits:

- The Complete Homeopathic/Bach Flower Essence Bathing Workshop
- The Complete Aromatherapy Bathing Workshop

The Dream-Maker:

- These eyelet-covered pillows are filled with dream-makers: Boxwood to induce "true dreams" of love, Herkimer diamonds to bring magical visionary dreams, and rose petals to soothe the heart.

Guided Meditation Tapes:

- *Journey to the Center of the Heart*
- *Inviting a Soul to Enter Your Life (Conceiving with Awareness)*
- *Journey to the Crystal Healing Pyramid*
- *Psychic Protection for the Spirit Travelers*

For ordering information, call:
Water Magic, Inc.
(203) 222-8854.

Index